grounded in prayer

A Small Group Training Guide for Congregational Prayer

Brent W. Dahlseng

Augsburg Fortress
Minneapolis

This resource is written in honor of four people who have a great heart for Jesus and have a love for the soil of life. Their love and dedication to living the Christian life have provided the seeds of faith for my family. I give thanks to God for my parents, Orville and Ruthe (Rosten) Dahlseng, and my wife Jody's parents, Milton and Carolyn (Huwe) Gumm.

—Brent W. Dahlseng

GROUNDED IN PRAYER
A Small Group Training Guide for Congregational Prayer

Developed in cooperation with the Division for Congregational Ministries of the Evangelical Lutheran Church in America, Brent W. Dahlseng, project leader.

Editors: Laurie J. Hanson and James Satter
Cover design: Marti Naughton
Cover and interior art: Greg Lewis Studios, copyright © 1998 Augsburg Fortress
Text design: James Satter

ISBN 0-8066-4676-4

07   06   05   4   5   6   7   8   9   10

Contents

Introduction

The "Parable of the Sower" in Mark 4:1-20 describes what happens when seed falls on four types of soil. In her book, *Sowing the Seed of the Gospel* (Philadelphia: Fortress Press, 1989), Mary Ann Tolbert says the stories in Mark 1-10 are best interpreted as examples of these types of soil.

Grounded in Prayer explores how prayer can be focused like a plow of the Holy Spirit to break up the hardhearted soil of the path, unseat the rocks of distraction, uproot the thorns and thistles of the world, and plant deeply the seed of faith in the good soil of the heart.

Week 1: The Groundwork of Prayer

The first week of this study introduces basic concepts, such as our need to pray, God's desire for us to pray, and consistency and persistence in prayer. This may be a review for some, but the daily practice of prayer may offer new ideas to others as well.

Week 2: Sharpening Your Personal Tools for Prayer

The second week builds on the foundation laid in the first week by exploring the different types of active prayer (adoration, confession of sin, thanksgiving, supplication, and worship).

Week 3: Praying for the Hardened Path

Resistance to the gospel is real. In the third week, your group will study and pray for a softening of hard hearts.

Week 4: Praying for the Rocky Ground

Many eager people come to our congregations, only to disappear into inactivity within a year or so. This study on the rocky ground will focus your prayer on all the distractions that get in the way when it comes to a life of faith.

Week 5: Praying for the Thorny Ground

When life gets difficult, we either turn to our faith or fall away from it. In this week we will look at these challenges to our faith.

Week 6: Blessing the Good Soil

How do we care for the good soil in our congregations, and bless it? This question is raised in the final week.

We all have samples of the four types of soil in our hearts and in our lives. *Grounded in Prayer* represents the joys and sorrows we have each faced in our lives. As we pray with compassion, just as Jesus ministered out of compassion, we can intercede or pray on behalf of people who have not seen the love, forgiveness, and new life in Jesus Christ. May our prayers for people who are "lost" bring forth the greatest joy in heaven, which comes about "over one sinner who repents" (Luke 15:7).

About the Study

Grounded in Prayer is an introductory study that uses individual daily prayer exercises and weekly small group sessions. No experience in prayer is necessary! This six-week study has three goals:

1. To deepen your personal prayer life and develop or strengthen your daily discipline of prayer and reading the Bible.
2. To be a tool for launching new prayer groups and strengthening existing groups.
3. To encourage the prayers of congregations.

Individual Daily Prayer Exercises

Like a garden, prayer requires daily attention. It cannot be practiced just once a week; it must take place every day. Some plants must be watered each day. Others, such as peas and tomatoes, need to be picked each day as they ripen. Weeds need to be hoed or picked out of the rows. God desires our daily prayers, as well as our attentive listening.

The individual prayer exercises will take an investment of 15 to 30 minutes per day. This may be a significant change in your busy life. Certainly, this time in study and prayer will impact your relationship with God.

Set a time and select a space to do this devotional work each day. As much as possible, keep to this schedule. There is great wisdom in establishing this time as close to the beginning of your day as possible. Otherwise, the work and distractions of the day tend to push our focus on God to the end of the day, when our best attention and energies may be spent. When you create an open window for God to break into your day by surrendering your schedule to God, you may discover possibilities that you would not find otherwise.

Note how each daily prayer exercise is laid out in three sections: READ, REFLECT, and RESPOND:

READ: This section explores the Bible text and the theme for the day.

REFLECT: Think about the questions and use the space provided to record your thoughts. If you need more writing space, use extra sheets of paper or a notebook or journal.

RESPOND: Consider taking action using the suggestions offered here.

The day after your small group first meets, begin with the daily prayer exercise for Week 1, Day 1. For example, if your initial meeting is held on a Tuesday evening, begin with the Day 1 exercise for Week 1 on Wednesday and continue to work through one exercise each day. In this example, the Day 7 exercise of Week 1 would be completed before the second small group meeting on the following Tuesday.

Weekly Small Group Sessions

Weekly sessions will allow you to discuss the six overall themes with others in your group and share what you have learned. This can be a blessing to everyone involved. The work you do in the daily exercises is crucial to these discussions.

As a member of the small group, you will need to commit to completing the daily prayer exercises, participating in each small group gathering, and praying for each person in your small group throughout this time together.

After the initial meeting of your small group, bring this book, a Bible, and a pen or pencil to each session.

Suggested ground rules for the small group

Discuss the following ground rules at the first meeting of your small group. (These ground rules are from *Anti-Racism Training Facilitator's Manual*, Lutheran Human Relations Association, 1998, p. 17.)

✦ Listen to each other's stories, giving each person full attention as they speak.

✦ Respect each person's journey, knowing that we are all at different places in relating to people who are different from ourselves, and that we can respect each person's place on that journey even when it differs from our own. People may disagree with what someone says, but it is important not to attack.

✦ No one can speak a third time until everyone has had a chance to speak once, since we want to be certain that everyone has a chance to speak.

✦ Be willing to share and grow, knowing that this is a safe place where what we say and feel will be respected.

✦ Speak only for yourself, sharing your own experiences and feelings, and not attempting to speak for or answer for any other person or group.

✦ Respect confidentiality as requested. You may share with others how you felt or what you learned, but it is important to keep confidential what is said in trust to the group.

Week 1

The Groundwork of Prayer

Mark 4:30-33

My Need to Pray

READ

The Holy Spirit works on God's behalf to woo people into a loving relationship with God through Christ our Lord. We learn truth about God and the deeper realities of the spiritual life through the scriptures and the sacraments. Based on this truth, we can also commune and communicate with God through prayer.

The parable of the mustard seed reminds us that many great things begin in small ways. This is also the case with a small prayer group. Through prayer, persistence and the power of the Holy Spirit, the movement of prayer can grow within individual lives and your congregation, much like the mustard tree.

The Bible helps us to understand how prayer-filled lives unfold. Through the stories of people such as Abraham (Genesis 12:1-5; 17:1-22), Moses (Exodus 3:1-4:17), the disciples (Mark 1:16-20), and Paul (Acts 9:1-18), we see that it is God who initiates the relationship with us. Martin Luther wrote about the work of the Holy Spirit:

> I believe that by own understanding or strength I cannot believe in Jesus Christ my Lord or come to him, but the Holy Spirit has called me by the gospel, enlightened me with his gifts, made me holy, and kept me in the true faith (*Luther's Small Catechism*, Third Article of the Apostles' Creed, Minneapolis: Augsburg Fortress, 1996, p. 23).

God calls us to pray. God's call to pray often begins as a general dissatisfaction with living a life focused on the "ruler of this world" (John 12:31; 14:30; 16:11). As we discover how unsatisfying the drive for wealth and worldly success really can be, the Holy Spirit begins to create a thirst within us for something more profound and real. The journey to know and be known by God begins. We begin to pray that God's will, not ours, will be done. We may have had glimpses of this spiritual path in our past or it may be a whole new adventure for us. Either way, the reality is the Holy Spirit leaves us unsettled until we seek and find our Creator and Savior, God.

Many are the voices that demand attention within our life. When Jesus, the Good Shepherd, calls us through the Holy Spirit (John 10:3-4), the destructive voices of the "ruler of this world" clamor for attention, fighting to keep us focused on self-centered ways of living (John 10:10). We should not be surprised by this inner battle within ourselves. Martin Luther said, "Temptation is of three kinds: of the flesh, the world, and the devil" (*Large Catechism*, *The Sixth Petition of the Lord's Prayer*, Kolb, Wengert edition). As we call on the name of the Lord, our self-centered flesh will die, the arguments of the world will fade, and the devil will recoil (1 Peter 5:8-9; James 2:19; Philippians 2:9-11). So, "Fight the good fight of the faith; take hold of the eternal life, to which you were called and for which you made the good confession in the presence of many witnesses" (1 Timothy 6:12).

REFLECT

Thomas Merton, a Trappist monk wrote, "If you have never had any distractions you don't know how to pray" (*New Seeds of Contemplation*, New York: New Directions, 1961, p. 221). The reality is that we all face various kinds of challenges in attempting to maintain a daily discipline of prayer.

1. What have been the obstacles for you in developing a consistent prayer life?

2. Reflect on some area of your life where you have had success maintaining a disciplined practice. (For example, an exercise program, housecleaning or shopping schedule, or financial-management plan.) What are the factors that make it possible for you to be consistent in these activities? What ideas might be applicable to your prayer life?

RESPOND

Prayer has a greater variety of expressions than any one of us discovers on our own. This is a gift the community of faith gives to us. It becomes exciting to learn from others as you continue to grow in prayer. Consider these words for prayer as you savor them.

RETURN—to God in prayer as you seek the presence of the Lord.

REMIT—(confess) your sin and trust in the promised forgiveness of Christ.

RECITE—your faith in God as you entrust your heart and prayer to Jesus.

REST—in the joy and peace of the presence of the Lord.

Psalm 8:3-8

God Needs and Wants You to Pray

READ

In the 18th century, one of the great leaders in prayer in the United States was a Methodist pastor named E. M. Bounds. He wrote:

> God needs prayer. . . . It is indispensable to God's work in the world.
> . . . Prayer is the great, universal force to advance God's cause; the
> reverence which hallows God's name; the ability to do God's will, and
> the establishment of God's kingdom in the hearts of the children. . . .
> and for the simple reason that by leaving prayer out of the catalogue
> of religious duties, we leave God out, and his work cannot progress
> without him" (*The Complete Works of E. M. Bounds on Prayer*, Grand
> Rapids: Baker, 1990, p. 379).

The will of God is clarified on earth through our prayers and accomplished through our actions and service. While we pray for God's will to be done, God may call us to act on that will.

Our Lord has commissioned and empowered us to be disciplemakers here on earth. Jesus' final words in Matthew's Gospel make this clear: "All authority in heaven and on earth has been given to me. Go therefore and make disciples of all nations" (Matthew 28:18-19a). Paul understood the power of prayer to initiate and empower this focus on discipleship: "I urge that supplications, prayers, intercessions, and thanksgivings be made for everyone, for kings and all who are in high positions. . . . This is right and is acceptable in the sight of God our Savior, who desires everyone to be saved and to come to the knowledge of the truth" (1 Timothy 2:1-4).

REFLECT

1. Read the following quote from Jane Vennard (*Intercessory Prayer: Praying for Friends and Enemies*, Minneapolis: Augsburg Fortress, 1995, p. 21) and explore your thoughts on why God both needs us to pray and has empowered us to pray for the salvation of all people on earth (Matthew 28:18-19a).

   By entering into intercessory prayer, we give God opportunities that God did not have before. As more people open themselves to God in prayer, God has more possibilities for responding to our needs. If God is to intervene in human affairs, if God is to continue to bring the creative power of love and justice into our lives, God needs us to pray and to act.

2. Who are the people that God is bringing to your heart to engage you in prayer? God can use us to pray for or intercede on behalf of others regarding their salvation. Is there anyone in particular for whom God may use you to intercede?

3. Prayer enables God to bring about change in lives and situations because of our spiritual authority on the earth to intercede and God's even greater desire to answer prayer. What are your thoughts as you reflect on this quote?

   Human beings have intervened in the heavenly liturgy. The uninterrupted flow of consequences is dammed for a moment. New alternatives become feasible. The unexpected becomes suddenly possible because people on earth have invoked heaven, the home of the possible, and have been heard. What happens next happens because people prayed (*Walter Wink, Engaging the Powers: Discernment and Resistance in a World of Domination*, Minneapolis: Augsburg Fortress, 1992, p. 299).

RESPOND

The Holy Spirit does not force anyone to believe in Jesus. Rather, the Holy Spirit invites, inspires, prompts, guides, and draws us to seek something more in our life. Our thirst for meaning will not be satisfied until we come to believe in Jesus as our Lord. As you pray for the individual or family that came to your mind in question 2 (above), visualize them in your prayers, asking God to unleash the Holy Spirit. What do you see as you pray?

❑ The beginning of an awareness of God.
❑ A crisis that becomes a crossroads to seeking God.
❑ A caring Christian neighbor who befriends them.
❑ A growing reality of powerlessness.
❑ A life becoming unmanageable.
❑ A realization of a hunger for something more.
❑ A desire to draw near to God.
❑ A heart openly thirsting for God in the midst of worship.
❑ Wrestling.
❑ A Christian mentor who listens, cares, and gives guidance.
❑ Joy in surrender.
❑ Passionately reaching out to others who are lost.

As you spend time in prayer for this situation, how is God calling you to respond? Where do you see yourself being used by the Holy Spirit in this relationship?

Matthew 7:7-8

The Imperative to Pray

READ

Prayer is the relational arm of our faith in God. Our relationship with God grows as we extend our faith through praying. As in any relationship, it takes time to develop your communication skills of listening and speaking. The more information you receive from another individual about him or herself, the better able you are to pull the stories together and gain an understanding of this person. Likewise, as you share your life story the other person learns more about you. The experiences you share together deepen your relationship further.

Study and spiritual reflection on the Bible teach us principles and truths about God and God's relationship with people. We gain information and understanding about God as we study and apply God's word in our life. God's word is the foundation upon which we can build a solid relationship with Jesus. Faith is grounded through reading and meditating on the scriptures.

In prayer, we exercise our faith, just as we strengthen our bodies through physical exercise. For any exercise program to have a lasting impact, it must be done regularly. For our prayer lives to grow and have an impact on our spiritual lives, prayer must be a consistent discipline in our life.

The most significant things you learn in life are often the result of mistakes or problems you have faced. Mistakes happen and are a natural part of your experience. If you see prayer in this way, you are released from the fear of making mistakes. Thomas Edison designed countless lightbulbs that *did not* produce light. Through his mistakes, Edison finally discovered how to make a lightbulb that worked.

Jesus commands us as his disciples to ask, search, and knock. The fear of praying wrongly can hold you back from experimenting and learning how to pray. It may be time to release yourself from the bondage of fear and begin exercising your faith by praying, so that you can continue to learn from God how to pray. Experiment. Ask the Holy Spirit to teach you how to pray, as the twelve disciples asked Jesus (Luke 11:1). Ask, search, and knock today.

REFLECT

Reflect on the following quote from Watchman Nee (*Let Us Pray*, translated from Chinese, New York: Christian Fellowship Publishing, 1977, p. 11):

> Prayer is the rail for God's work. Indeed, prayer is to God's will as rails are to a train. The locomotive is full of power: it is capable of running a thousand miles a day. But if there are no rails, it cannot move forward a single inch.

1. What does this metaphor for prayer suggest to you about God's command for us to pray?

2. Name the fears that might be holding you back from praying with confidence. What can help you to overcome those fears?

3. The twelve disciples asked Jesus to teach them how to pray. Because prayer is experiential and you learn as you pray, experiment with these suggestions, which offer a variety of physical postures for prayer.

Feet and legs

Kneel (Psalm 95:6; Ephesians 3:14; Matthew 2:11)
Lie prostrate (Deuteronomy 9:18, 25; Psalm 38:6)
Stand (Psalm 22:23; 24:3; 33:8; 134:1)
Dance (Psalm 30:11; 149:3; 150:4; Ecclesiastes 3:4; Jeremiah 31:13)
Walk (Psalm 26:3, 11; 56:13; 81:13; 86:11; 116:9)
Leap (2 Samuel 6:16; Acts 3:8)

Hands and arms

Hands open (a posture of receptivity)
Arms open (Hebrew posture of prayer)
Folded hands (a posture to avoid distraction, especially for young children)
Hands and arms raised (Exodus 9:29,33; Psalm 134:2; Psalm 141:2; Psalm 143:6)

Head

Head raised (Psalm 3:3; 24:7, 9)
Head bowed (Psalm 35:13; 95:6; 138:2)

Eyes

Eyes open (Psalm 25:15; 123:1-2; 145:15)
Eyes closed (to keep our minds from distraction, especially for young children)

Voice

Silent, still (Psalm 46:10; 62:1,5)
Shout (Joshua 6:5; Ezra 3:11; Psalm 47:1; 65:13; 71:23; 132:16)
Sing (Psalm 5:11; 7:17; 9:2, 11; 13:6; 98:1, 4-5, 8)
Rhythmic speaking (prayer that is liturgical in style)
Laughter (Job 8:21; Psalm 126:2; Ecclesiastes 3:4)

Breathing

Breathe in—(and say under your breath) "Come, Holy Spirit, Come"

Breathe out—your worries, frustrations, anger, and complacency

Breathe in—"Light of Christ"

Breathe out—all darkness and fears

Breathe in—"Peace, be still"

Breathe out—all anxieties

RESPOND

There is no right way to pray using your body. Try these postures for prayer a number of times privately. It might feel awkward to try anything new with your body, just as it feels awkward when you are learning to dance. Take time to experience the connection between body posture and your expression in prayer. Which postures for prayer feel most comfortable to you?

Mark 14:35-36

Keeping God at the Center of Prayer

READ

One of the challenges of prayer is that our relationship with God is between us, as created beings, and God, our creator. Jesus describes God's relationship with us in prayer as being like a parent who wants to give the best and most helpful gifts to his or her child (Matthew 7:9-11).

You may have had the experience of praying for someone or something and not receiving what you prayed for. This experience can be so derailing that it causes some to stop praying. God does desire to give you good gifts and promises to answer your prayers. But just as parents sometimes see that granting a child's request will not be in the child's best interest or in the interest of others, we see in part here on earth, but God sees all situations with clarity (1 Corinthians 13:12).

We must remember in our praying to stay focused on God. Jesus was heavy-hearted when he came before God in Gethsemane. Yet in the midst of his agony, he released his situation and sought the will of the heavenly Creator. Jesus shows us that we can and should bring all the requests and situations that are on our hearts to God. Jesus honored and kept God and God's will at the center of his prayer. Jesus teaches us, in his prayer in the garden of Gethsemane, that the main focus of our prayer is not us, but God. God is the main thing. God, who sees clearly all the implications of our situation, knows what is best.

Some might argue, "If God is going to do whatever God wants to do anyway, then why bother praying?" Consider these two thoughts.

First, God needs us to pray for and serve God's will here on earth. Second, God is moved by our prayers (Genesis 18:22-32; Mark 7:24-30).

Being people who practice prayer in our lives is a learning experience. Because our understanding is limited, there will be prayers that seem to go unanswered, without a clear answer as to "why." We may come to understand the answer to our prayer later in time, or we may never know the answer. Keeping God at the center is key to our faith and our prayers. No matter what, may God's will be accomplished through our willingness and obedience to be used in prayer.

REFLECT

Prayer is definitely a discipline. If it is going to consistently be a part of our lives, most of us will have to be intentional about our prayer life. This begins by establishing a set time to pray.

✦ Set aside your best available time during the day, not simply when you fall exhausted into bed at the end of the day.

✦ Give prayer priority time. Honor your commitment to that time with God in prayer.

1. Keep in mind the natural rhythm of your day (or night, if you are a shift worker). A possible prayer rhythm might look like this:

✦ Awaken—surrender your day and offer prayers of thanksgiving to God.

✦ Breakfast—read and pray over a scripture passage.

✦ Mid-morning or as you commute to work—examine your heart and confess your sins to God.

✦ Lunch or noon—revisit and pray through the scripture passage you focused on at breakfast.

✦ Mid-afternoon or evening commute—prayers on behalf of others.

✦ Dinner or supper—revisit the scripture text once again, being especially attentive to the voice of God.

✦ Bedtime—prayers of surrender, personal petitions, and prayers seeking the peace of God.

2. Although you can pray anywhere, there may be advantages to having a set place for prayer within your home. Some homes have space set aside for an entertainment center. Why not create a prayer corner that will remind you to pray? This may be as simple as a corner shelf that could hold an icon of Christ, a cross, and a candle. If you have room for a small table, you could add a place for your Bible, devotional book, prayer list, spiritual journal, and so on. Do you want to create a sacred space for prayer in your home? If so, what could you include in this space?

RESPOND

A prayer covenant is a way of committing yourself to God. Consider the prayer covenant on page 128 as an example. A prayer covenant can be revised and expanded as circumstances change. Take a moment to write your own prayer covenant and live with it for a time. Revise it when needed.

Luke 18:1-8

Persist in Prayer

READ

Margaret has come through numerous difficulties in life, yet through the pain God has continued to be active in restoring her to health. She has played a part in this process of healing because she continued to seek God and to invest herself in the hard work of extended counseling. What Margaret demonstrated most of all was persistence to seek God's strength to be as healthy and whole as possible. Prayer was an integral part of this whole process.

Jesus told the parable of the persistent widow so that we would "pray always and not lose heart" (Luke 18:1). Will God not hear and answer those who "cry to him day and night?" (Luke 18:7). This parable encourages us to continually bring our prayers before God.

In the United States and other economically prosperous nations, few of us know what it means to be desperate. As a result, many churches have lost the passion for local and global mission. Apathy toward those within our communities who or are "lost" in terms of faith is evident across denominational lines. Few people persist in prayer, yet this is exactly what Jesus calls us to do.

During times of great persecution or need, churches have risen up and accomplished great feats of missionary and evangelical work. With the onslaught of school shootings, teenage suicides, drug and alcohol abuse, our culture is crying out for a lost sense of meaning. Many people are seeking meaning in their lives. We must respond obediently to Jesus in this time and persist in prayer. God is calling the Christian church back to its roots, to rediscover the gospel imperative for us to be bold witnesses who rely on the power of prayer. Do we have the will to respond?

REFLECT

1. Margaret's story is not unique. Many people in our congregations and communities live the pain of brokenness. In your life, which people are experiencing some significant pain? How will you connect with these individuals, and how will you pray for them?

2. Jesus said that we are to "pray always and not lose heart." Many of us enter into prayer as "sprinters" who offer prayers once but then move on to new prayer requests. It takes the endurance of a long-distance runner to persist in our prayers as Jesus suggests. What will you need to grow in your endurance in prayer?

3. Congregations go through a life cycle: birth, growth, plateau, decline, and death. Has your congregation lost its passion for those in your community who do not know and worship Jesus? By the power of the Holy Spirit, congregations can be turned around and restored. What is your prayer for your congregation?

RESPOND

Ask Jesus to show you for whom to pray. Read Luke 15 and notice what brings the greatest joy in heaven! Pray through the parable of the lost sheep, the lost coin, and the lost son. If you ask, God will bring someone into your life for whom you are to pray and be a witness.

1 Thessalonians 5:16-18

Pray without Ceasing

READ

Have you driven along a narrow and winding road at night that required your full attention to travel safely? If so, you know how much energy it takes to focus that intently on the road.

Jesus talked about two roads in life: one is wide and the other is narrow. It is the narrow road that leads to eternal life: ". . . for the gate is wide and the road is easy that leads to destruction, and there are many who take it. For the gate is narrow and the road is hard that leads to life, and there are few who find it" (Matthew 7:13-14).

Just as a narrow and winding road requires our full attention while driving, praying without ceasing requires our full attention on God. How is it even remotely possible to *rejoice always, pray without ceasing,* and *give thanks in all circumstances* (1 Thessalonians 5:16-18)? Paul is calling us here to be conscious of God's presence. To live a "God-conscious" life means that we are increasingly aware of the fact that God is always with us and has a daily plan for our lives. A faithful husband carries the thought of his wife with him wherever he goes. In all of his conversations and actions, even though he may not bring his wife into the conversation, he is ever aware that he is a married man. He honors his wife by the way that he enters into and withdraws from other conversations.

Being God-conscious is an awareness that we belong to Jesus and that he too is with us in everything we say and do. Is this conversation pleasing to him? Is it filled with compassion and care toward coworkers or neighbors? If it is not, this is a time to call on Jesus' name and ask for his guidance. As Christians, we have the added blessing of being able to talk with our Lord, even though he is not physically present. We can ask for advice and wisdom in the midst of work decisions, conversations, and various aspects of our day.

Finally, you can pray to see God blessing a coworker who is having a miserable day. You can ask God for ideas at work and see what God brings to your mind. These are genuine prayers. Begin to engage your imagination to help you see God at work in a person's life or in a problem situation.

When you think of prayer, perhaps you think of words and sentences. To pray without ceasing requires you to move beyond words, at times, into a simple awareness of the Lord's presence. You can use your God-inspired imagination once again to take the reality of the Lord's presence with you deeper into your day.

REFLECT

1. Ephesians 3:20-21 reads, "Now to him who by the power at work within us is able to accomplish abundantly far more than we can ask or imagine, to him be glory in the church and in Christ Jesus to all generations, forever and ever. Amen." You will know the difference between God-inspired imagination and your own self-centered imagination because God comes to build up, encourage, and comfort those in need. Use passages such as Ephesians 3:20-21 to ask yourself, "What is God placing on my mind?"

2. Paul prayed for the Christians at the church in Ephesus: "I pray that the God of our Lord Jesus Christ, the Father of glory, may give you a spirit of wisdom and revelation as you come to know him, so that, with the eyes of your heart enlightened, you may know the hope to which he has called you" (Ephesians 1:17-18).

Ask God to let the eyes of your heart see more clearly. Pray a simple prayer like this: "Show me your presence, Lord, as I go through my day. May I know and do your will. Use me to be a servant to others." How are you becoming more aware of God throughout each day?

3. God is love and desires us to be filled with love. Is there someone you are to shower with love this week? How will you show this person the love of Christ?

RESPOND

To be aware of God at all times and in all places, first ask the Lord's presence into your workplace, car, home, and so on. Second, try to place reminders to pray throughout your home or workplace. In one congregation, small green adhesive dots were distributed to worshippers. Each person placed a green dot on his or her watch. Now every time the people look at their watches, the green dots serve as reminders to pray. Others call to mind the picture of Christ standing at the door, knocking. Every time they enter a doorway, they are reminded to pray. How will you remind yourself to pray without ceasing?

Isaiah 59:15-16; Ezekiel 22:30

Called to Intercede

READ

You cannot and should not attempt to stand alone in intercession. Paul, the great missionary to the Gentiles, repeatedly asked for the intercessions of the church (Ephesians 6:19-20; Colossians 4:3; 1 Thessalonians 5:25; 2 Thessalonians 3:1). Jesus took his closest disciples with him to the garden of Gethsemane, to intercede for him (Matthew 26:36-46). You will need the prayers of other individuals or a prayer group as you intercede for the people and situations that the Lord places on your heart.

We have access to God in prayer because of our identity in Christ Jesus. He gives us access because his blood on the cross makes us stand reconciled before God: "It is Christ Jesus, who died, yes, who was raised, who is at the right hand of God, who indeed intercedes for us" (Romans 8:34). Jesus stands before God and says, "Listen to this person, for she is one of mine." Also, "there is also one mediator between God and humankind, Christ Jesus" (1 Timothy 2:5). We are encouraged to pray in the name of our savior, redeemer, and intercessor, Jesus Christ. We have been called to intercede for the needs of the world (1 Timothy 2:1-4). God does not force issues on earth but rather works through the prayers and service of the faithful. Consider this definition:

> Intercessory prayer is an extension of the ministry of Jesus through His Body, the Church, whereby we mediate between God and humanity for the purpose of reconciling the world to Him, or between Satan and humanity for the purpose of enforcing the victory of Calvary (Dutch Sheets, *Intercessory Prayer*, Ventura, California: Regal Books, 1996, p. 42).

Your intercessions in prayer on behalf of others are important for the accomplishment of the Lord's will on earth: "Your kingdom come, your will be done, on earth as it is in heaven" (Matthew 6:10). Be encouraged! Persist! May the will of the Lord be accomplished through the intercessions of Jesus' body, the church.

REFLECT

1. As you grow in your prayer life, you will find yourself moving beyond the needs of your family, your circle of friends, and into prayers for even those people you do not know personally. As you read these verses, for whom are you encouraged to pray?

   Matthew 5:44
   Matthew 9:36-38
   Luke 22:31-32
   Luke 23:34
   John 17:1-26

2. The Bible is filled with prayers of intercession that can serve as excellent models for your growth in prayer. Look at the following prayers and note what you observe about them.

   Exodus 32:11-12
   Colossians 1:9-13
   Daniel 9:17-19
   1 Samuel 12:23

3. For whom should you pray? Consider this: "There is no more important ministry in the church than the ministry of intercessory prayer. A multitude of people need your prayer. Remember your pastor, other leaders in the church, and all those who share in your life in the congregation. The strength of the fellowship and ministry in any congregation is heavily dependent upon this ministry of prayer on behalf of one another" (Richard Beckmen, *Prayer: Beginning Conversations with God*, Minneapolis: Augsburg Fortress, 1995, p. 37).

RESPOND

Do whatever works for you to remember those for whom you are called to pray. Many people find it helpful to use a prayer list. This is simply a numbered list that includes the name of the person, their specific request, and the date that you received this request. For example:

1. Jane Doe, for healing from breast cancer, 3/1/2002.
2. Jim Smith, that he may be able to find work, 4/17/2002.

Pray for each request on your prayer list until you either hear that it has been answered or receive inner assurance that your intercessions are complete. One of the frustrations of intercessory prayer is not hearing how the prayer was answered. Release these frustrations into the hands of the Lord, who has answered your prayers. Above all, keep on praying!

Week 2

Sharpening Your Personal Tools for Prayer

Start Praying

READ

There is only one way to begin gardening in the spring and that is to sharpen up the tools, get out there, and get to work! Many people experience great joy in turning over the soil and readying it for the day when it is time to begin planting the seeds for a new year.

Just as it is important for a gardener to have tools that are ready for use, so too it is important for those of us who are going to engage in prayer to sharpen our skills by practicing prayer. There is a difference between being well informed about prayer and being someone who prays. This book presents a variety of styles of prayer to help you find the practices that work best for you.

We will look at how to become grounded in prayer as we study the four types of soil in the parable of the sower in Mark 4. The four types of soil in the parable represent our receptivity to the message of Mark's Gospel. Some areas of our life may be very resistant to the seed of the gospel, like the soil of the hardened path. Other areas of our life may be very responsive initially, but when life becomes challenging, the roots of faith are not deep and it withers and dies. Another type of soil is like the thorny area of the garden. The seeds that fall in this soil sprout and grow, but eventually they are choked out by the lures of the world. Finally, there is the good soil that produces increase.

REFLECT

1. As you think about addressing God in prayer, which images of God are most helpful to you? See the list of images on page 32.

- ❑ God who provides: Genesis 22:14
- ❑ The Lord who heals: Exodus 15:26
- ❑ The Lord our Maker: Psalm 95:6
- ❑ Hen gathering her brood: Matthew 23:37
- ❑ Light of the World: John 8:12
- ❑ Gate: John 10:7
- ❑ Good shepherd: John 10:11
- ❑ The Way: John 14:6
- ❑ The Truth: John 14:6
- ❑ The Life: John 14:6
- ❑ Other: _____

2. Pray over the brief prayer of Jabez:

   Oh that you would bless me and enlarge my border,
   and that your hand would be with me,
   and that you would keep me from hurt and harm!
   —1 Chronicles 4:10

Are you ready for Jesus to enlarge your spiritual territory of influence and responsibility? Asking for Jesus' hand to be upon you is seeking God's greater anointing for ministry. Another translation of the last part of the prayer divides it up into two petitions: "Keep me from evil. That I may not cause pain." This petition sounds very close to the petition "and deliver us from evil" in the Lord's Prayer. Is the prayer of Jabez a helpful model as you pray for yourself and others? Why or why not?

RESPOND

Having a prayer partner can be a wonderful gift for prayer as well as accountability. Do you already have a prayer partner to call or pray with at least once a week? If not, who could be that partner for you?

Preparing Your Heart to Pray

READ

After a garden is designed and laid out, the work of tilling the soil begins. This step of turning over and loosening the soil enables plants to grow to greater productivity. Numerous hand tools and power tools can assist the gardener in loosening and aerating the soil, but the labor-intensive and time-consuming work leaves the gardener feeling very stiff and sore in the following days.

We have all experienced relationships that have broken down, and where communication has stalled. Ignoring the problem and starting over again seldom brings lasting results. Like the work of tilling the soil of your garden, humbling yourself and admitting your part in the problem is both hard work and painful. But the healing that results is essential for a healthy relationship.

Not only did King David force an affair on Bathsheba, but he also tried to cover it up. When this plot failed, David planned the murder of Bathsheba's husband. God sent the prophet Nathan to reveal David's sin and expose his hardened heart. As a result, David humbled himself, admitted his sins, confessed them to God, and desired to change his ways (repent).

Psalm 51 is a theological gem! In the psalm, David pleads for God's mercy (verses 1-2), then acknowledges and confesses his sin (verses 3-5). He finds himself spiritually crushed and in misery (verses 8-9). The culminating point (verses 10-12) describes the "clean heart principle":

✦ Being made clean requires open, willing, and honest confession and repentance (verses 7 and 10).

✦ Repentance also implies a desire to change sinful ways. David asked God to put a new and right spirit within him (verse 10) and sought a willing and generous heart to sustain him (verse 12). He was guilty of a forced affair and murder. Now, in contrast, David desired to have a generous and giving heart. That's a change of attitude!

✦ In joy and thanksgiving for God's grace, David took action to reach and serve others. The beginning of a changed life is living in gratitude as a servant of God: "Then I will teach transgressors your ways, and sinners will return to you" (verse 13).

Prepare to pray for others by asking the Holy Spirit to guide you in an examination of your heart. Seek a clean heart when you enter into intercession for others because "like a roaring lion your adversary the devil prowls around, looking for someone to devour" (1 Peter 5:8). Satan knows the weaknesses, sins, and insecurities that can derail you from praying. The two key attitudes for those who pray for others are humility and repentance. Live in Jesus' forgiving grace!

REFLECT

1. Read and contemplate what these Bible passages are saying to you: Proverbs 28:13; Hebrews 4:16; and Hebrews 10:19-22.

2. Pray: *Gracious God, you have searched me and known me. I ask you to reveal to me my sins that I might confess them, repent of them, and seek your wisdom and strength to bring about the change in my life that you desire, in Jesus' name. Amen*

Record what God brings to your mind in response to this prayer. Be still and wait for the Lord to speak:

RESPOND

Responding to an area of sin in your life by taking positive action will empower change. What action do you want to take this week?

Psalm 63:1-4

Seeking the Presence of God in Worship

READ

Gardening tools that are properly cared for save much time and labor in the long run. A dull spade or hoe requires much more effort to use than one that is properly sharpened. Some tools need to be sharpened after every two or three hours of use.

Nothing will sharpen your tools for prayer as much as the regular worship of Jesus. The hard work of prayer can wear down the faith and hope of the one who prays. We need to be renewed, both individually and corporately, by taking time to enter into the presence of God and worship the Lord. The psalmist characterizes this need as a dire thirst and seeks the Lord. Then the psalmist begins to worship and praise God by affirming truths about the Lord: "Because your steadfast love is better than life, my lips will praise you" (Psalm 63:3). When we feel dry of God, affirming truths about the Lord will release the presence of God within us and water our thirsty soul. The psalmist adds, "my soul is satisfied as with a rich feast" (63:5).

In addition to the richness of the psalms for worship and praise, we have been blessed with historic hymns as well as contemporary praise and worship songs. Play your favorite praise music at home or in the car as a tool to sing and worship the Lord. Rejoice in the Lord who loves you, cares for your every need, forgives you, and desires to renew and strengthen you. Invite God's presence and receive all that God wants to give you as you express yourself in worship. Free yourself to express a full range of love toward God.

We can also quiet ourselves and simply be in the presence of the Lord. We live in such a noisy world that being still in the presence of God can be a powerful time of refreshment for our hearts. Slowly and silently meditate on Jesus. Eventually, you may be able to simply be in God's presence without even needing to say a word.

The psalmist writes, "in the shadow of your wings I sing for joy" (63:7). Let us seek and draw near to our Lord, like a chick under the wing of the mother hen. There we will find peace and joy in the loving presence of the Lord.

REFLECT

Read and reflect on these passages as they relate to worshiping the Lord and write down your thoughts or questions: Exodus 33:7-11; Psalm 27:7-8, 13-14; Psalm 62:5-7; Psalm 100; and Psalm 105:1-6.

RESPOND

✦ Study the Bible to learn more about how God desires to be worshiped. Look at how words such as these are used in the Bible: presence, worship, praise, and rejoice. (Use a Bible dictionary or concordance for this. One of these may be provided in the back of your Bible.)

✦ Find out more about the way your congregation worships God. Why does your church worship in the style that it does?

✦ Explore why other denominations worship God in the way that they do.

✦ Make time to worship on your own each day.

Psalm 92:1-3

Give Thanks

READ

Gardening is much easier now than in the past. From cultivators, chippers, and shredders, to string trimmers, lawn mulchers, and mowers, advances in power tools have made soil preparation and lawn care much easier than it was in the past.

There is much in life that we overlook and take for granted. This can impair our perspective on life and cause us to focus on problems rather than on the One who provides for us and guides us through the troubled waters of life. Those who wallow in self-pity are robbed of energy. Meanwhile, an attitude filled with gratitude toward life and God releases positive energy within you. Knowing that thanksgiving releases joy within us, why do we so quickly forget to thank God each day?

God desires our thanksgiving. We are told, "Enter his gates with thanksgiving, and his courts with praise. Give thanks to him, bless his name" (Psalm 100:4). In addition, every life situation is reason to give God thanks (1 Thessalonians 5:18). As individuals, families, and congregations we can renew our hearts by taking inventory of our lives and discovering all there is for which to be thankful.

Give thanks to God for other people, and let them know they are in your prayers of thanksgiving. Too many people have not heard enough good spoken about them or how another person loves them. Imagine the power that could be released if people heard that prayers are offered to God on their behalf, thanking God for bringing them into this life and expressing God's love for them. Think about the impact one Sunday school teacher could have if he or she spent time in prayer thanking God for the class and for the gift of each student, by name.

How can you take this concept of the power of prayers of thanksgiving and apply it in your congregation? At the very least, make prayers of thanksgiving a common practice among all congregational groups: the council, committees, choirs, bands, small groups, confirmation classes, and so on. Creatively find ways to express thanksgiving for those near you.

REFLECT

1. What characteristics of God are you most thankful for?

❑ Loving   ❑ Compassionate

❑ Gracious   ❑ Creative

❑ Merciful   ❑ Life-giving

❑ Slow to anger   ❑ Eternal

❑ Forgiving   ❑ Other:_____

❑ Same yesterday, today, and forever

2. What are you most thankful for in your own life?

❑ Family   ❑ Health

❑ Friends   ❑ Sight

❑ Home   ❑ Hearing

❑ Church   ❑ Sense of smell

❑ Work or vocation   ❑ Sense of touch

❑ Ability to taste and enjoy good food

❑ Ability to travel and see the world

❑ God's claim on your life as a redeemed child

❑ Other:_____

RESPOND

✦ Write a poem or song, or paint a picture, that expresses your gratitude to God.

✦ Being thankful is contagious. Encourage others by sharing your thanksgiving for life.

✦ In your prayers, joyfully express your gratitude to God.

Philippians 4:6-7

Praying for Yourself

READ

> *If you are not active all week and then do heavy manual labor in a garden on the weekend, you risk back strain or injury. However, you can help to prevent stiffness and injury by warming up your muscles before you begin working, bending correctly, and using your leg muscles as much as possible during any lifting. Taking care of yourself in these ways is an important part of gardening.*

Taking care of yourself is also important in your prayer life. One of the prevailing misconceptions about prayer is that you are to pray only for others and not for yourself. Intercessory prayer for others is a gift and you receive a great deal in return for such prayers, but your personal prayers of petition are equally important.

God desires to hear your prayers for yourself as much as your intercessory prayers for others. Because God loves you, you can entrust your personal needs into Jesus' hands. You can bring both your petitions for yourself as well as the intercessions that God has laid on your heart. All the while, a balance must be maintained between personal petitions and intercessions. Otherwise, you run the risk of becoming so focused on yourself that you fail to see God's bigger picture or so focused on others that you do not deal with your own needs and concerns.

To believe that God will meet your needs requires a more personal act of faith than praying for the needs of others. Further, when you experience answers to prayer in your own life, this can build your faith that God answers prayer and give you more confidence as you intercede for others. If you seek the will of God and expect to see answers in your personal petitions, you practice what you encourage others to believe.

REFLECT

Prayerfully consider these Bible passages where individuals cried out to God in their time of need: Psalm 17:6-7; Psalm 31:14-17; Psalm 88:13-14; Psalm 116:1-6; Psalm 118:5-9; Psalm 141:1; Psalm 142.

RESPOND

Create a list of your personal prayer requests. Date your requests, bring them before the Lord, and record answers as they are received. You can revise this list as needed over time.

Personal Prayer Requests		
Date	**Personal Request**	**Answer Received**

1 Samuel 3:1-10

Listening Prayer

READ

Successful gardeners know there will always be additional work beyond preparing the soil, planting, watering, and harvesting the produce. Part of this work includes frequent weeding, caring for plants that suffer from various threats, and responding to special challenges as they arise. Gardening requires frequent attention.

Prayer requires attention to God. To those who seek God with an open heart and mind and are attentive to God's voice, God still speaks. How do we hear from God? God speaks to us through the scriptures and the sacraments of Baptism and Communion. As we see in the Bible, some people also receive visions, dreams, and ideas from God.

We must remember, though, that the many thoughts clamoring for our attention make it difficult to discern God's voice. The majority of our thoughts are the result of information gained from our five senses: what we see, hear, taste, touch, and smell. There are also negative and destructive thoughts that criticize and tear down others as well as ourselves.

The following suggestions can help us discern and know the voice of the Lord.

First, consider whether a new thought or idea is in alignment with the scriptures.

Second, seek the advice of your pastor, spiritual director, or another trusted and wise Christian.

Third, take comfort in the fact that it took Samuel four times before he learned that it was the Lord calling to him. God will continue to communicate to your receptive heart.

It is possible to begin to recognize God's voice because God gives guidance and direction for you and others for whom you are interceding. Jesus said, "When the Spirit of truth comes, he will guide you into all truth; for he will not speak on his own, but will speak whatever he hears, and he will declare to you the things that are to come" (John 16:13). Jesus assured his disciples, as he assures us, that the Holy Spirit will guide us and be his vehicle for communication. In addition, the Holy Spirit will speak words that build up, encourage, and console you as well as others (1 Corinthians 14:3).

Have you heard from God? Perhaps you have stopped by to visit someone you were not planning to visit, only to discover that you were needed there at that time. Or, the person cutting your hair, without knowing it, spoke words confirming some action that you were planning to take. Or, a Bible verse keeps coming to mind or has new meaning for you. These are examples of learning to know and listen to the voice of God.

In intercessory prayer, it is a gift from God to receive specific thoughts on how to pray for a person or situation. This may start with an impression that a person is hurting or in pain. As you pray, focusing on that impression of pain, how God wants you to pray for the situation may become clearer to you. This is a process of learning to receive and know the voice of God. If the person is present as you are praying for them, you can ask questions for more clarity. You seldom learn without risking a mistake. Based on the person's response, you continue to pray.

God still speaks. Are you willing to listen?

REFLECT

In *The Pocket Guide to Prayer*, Gary Egeberg suggests six ways to improve your listening prayer skills (Minneapolis: Augsburg Fortress, 1999, pp. 52-54). Pray and reflect on each of these:

1. Strive for an attitude that expects God to communicate.
2. Express your desire to listen and have a two-way relationship to God.
3. Experiment with prayer postures and gestures that reflect your openness to receiving and hearing God's voice.
4. Begin your time in prayer by becoming quiet and slowing down.
5. Allow for some silence in your life, particularly during times of prayer.
6. Unload your concerns into God's care. This can be helpful before a time of silence.

RESPOND

As you begin to listen to God, or even if you are experienced in listening prayer, consider recording the thoughts, dreams, or ideas that God sends to you. A reflective journal can be helpful in learning to discern God's voice. (Give journaling a 30-day trial before you dismiss the idea.) Use the space below or a separate journal.

Psalm 3:1-4

Answered Prayer

READ

The seasoned gardener knows the value of keeping a record of the successes from each year of gardening. This record enables the gardener to plan more effectively for the next year. What plant grew best in which soil? What variety of green beans was the most productive in this garden?

One of the biggest challenges facing someone involved in intercessory prayer is the question of whether or not your prayers were answered. All people who pray are in a learning mode. We all need encouragement to continue in our enthusiasm for prayer. It can be encouraging to record answers to prayer when you are aware of them.

If you regularly pray for requests from strangers, you will seldom receive responses regarding answers to these prayers. This can become discouraging. How can you receive encouragement to continue intercessory prayers? Consider the following ideas:

✦ Read and meditate frequently on scripture passages that remind us that God hears and answers prayer.

✦ Find a prayer partner with whom you can meet at least weekly to pray together. You and your partner can serve as encouragers to each other.

✦ Invite others from your congregation to gather for regular intercessory prayer meetings. (*The Grounded in Prayer Leader Guide* contains suggestions for establishing a prayer service in your congregation.)

◆ Send a letter to other churches in your community to gather for a special intercessory prayer service. This may rotate among the churches, meeting up to two or four times a year. Larger community-wide services of prayer can provide real encouragement to everyone involved.

◆ Develop a Sunday bulletin insert that members of the congregation can use periodically to request prayers and record answers to prayer. At the bottom of the sheet, assure those filling out the information that the requests and answers to prayer will be kept confidential unless otherwise indicated.

◆ Read answers to prayer at a prayer service so that thanksgiving to God can be expressed. (Read only answers to prayers that are not confidential.)

◆ Invite those who have experienced answers to prayer to write a brief note of thanksgiving for the congregation's newsletter, if they are comfortable doing this.

◆ Invite those who have experienced answers to prayer to give a brief testimonial during a worship service.

REFLECT

Read and meditate frequently on these Bible passages that speak of answered prayer. Look for other Bible verses, hymns, poems, and testimonials to answered prayer as well.

1 Samuel 1:26-27
Ezra 8:21-23
Nehemiah 1:4-6; 9:27
Psalm 6:6-9
Psalm 18:6
Psalm 34:4
Psalm 66:19
Psalm 118:21
1 John 5:14-15

RESPOND

✦ Keep a prayer journal. In one section, record Bible verses that speak of answered prayer. In another section, list dated answers to prayer.

✦ Thank God for answers to prayer that you became aware of in the last week or month.

✦ Find ways to encourage others by sharing answers to prayer.

~~Unknown~~ Virginia

Sanders → Family Friend Santon

D. Davis - Cousin w/ Bad Diagnosis
Bill

J. Jason's Brother & Sister in law in Kenya
Brian   Katie

M - Healing & Answers for Melissa's Health

T - Friends with no income fundn jobs Bill & Michelle
Hus sistr

K.   Family

D. Tommy & Elizabeth

Week 3

Praying for the Hardened Path

The Path

READ

In her book *Praying the Parables* (Downers Grove, Illinois: InterVarsity Press, 1996), Joyce Huggett provides insight into what generally happened to any seed that fell on the path:

> First-century Palestinian farmers possess not whole fertile fields, but strips of terraced land that are partitioned off by stone walls. Access is gained to a succession of these strips of land by means of a narrow, unplowed, hard-packed, protected public right-of-way: the path. No farmer throws seeds on the path. This farmer sows seed along the path. The soil along or adjacent to the path is inhospitable. Farmers try to cultivate it, but it's impossible. This is where they back and turn the oxen that pull the cumbersome plow. There is no way that the ground here can be plowed or harrowed. Even so, the farmer in Jesus' story takes the risk of sowing precious seed right there (p. 42).

As you begin to explore how to pray for receptive soil in the hearts of others, you must begin by searching your own heart. As we saw in Week 2, the work of prayer must begin with your own life of faith. In terms of receptivity to Christ, we as believers are made up of a mixture of the types of soil mentioned in the parable of the sower. In much of our life, we may be very receptive soil. In other areas of our life, we may have very thinly rooted faith. In still other areas, our faith may be choked out or the soil may be entirely resistant to faith. Areas of resistance to Jesus might include pride, unwillingness to forgive, or persistent sin. After you have done the hard work of examination, repentance, and confession of your sins, you can begin to use your God-inspired imagination to pray for the hardened soil or hard-heartedness in others.

The first-century Palestinian farmer could not break up the soil along the path with his plow, but the plow of the Holy Spirit knows no limits. In fact, "for God all things are possible" (Mark 10:27). As you pray for someone who is hard-hearted, you can prayerfully visualize the sharpened plow of the Spirit beginning to cut through the callused heart of this particular individual.

It may take a long time to see an answer to these prayers. Persist in your prayers believing that, in time, the Holy Spirit will break through the hardened soil of the heart and make it receptive to the softening rain of the Spirit. Eventually, this person may be receptive to the life-changing power of Jesus Christ, and come to believe in him as their Lord and Savior. One of the criminals crucified with Jesus became repentant as he was dying on a cross (Luke 23:39-43). It is a matter of time before the will of God is accomplished, as we pray for people who are hard-hearted!

As you pray for someone else, remember that God alone knows the heart of each person. Be careful not to talk publicly about a person's "hard-heartedness" because this can cause unintended hurt to the person for whom you are praying. We can only pray in accordance with our best understanding and leave the rest to be discerned by the Spirit (Romans 8:26-27).

REFLECT

Repentance and confession enable the Holy Spirit to soften our hearts and prepare us to intercede for others. Such honesty with God and ourselves connects us to God. We are then ready to pray for people who are hard-hearted. (You may want to review the Week 2, Day 2 exercise at this time.)

1. Read John 8:1-11. Jesus said, "Let anyone among you who is without sin be the first to throw a stone at her" (8:7). This comment by Jesus disarmed all the men who were poised to stone the woman who had been caught in the act of adultery. As you pray for others, you too must be disarmed of a judgmental spirit. When you consider praying for a particular person, ask yourself why and watch for any personal agendas.

2. Think about a time when you were judgmental about someone else. How did this influence your prayers?

RESPOND

What are the characteristics of hard-heartedness? In Luke 6:43-45, the heart is known by the "fruit" it produces. Read Galatians 5:18-23 for a list of the works of the flesh and the fruits of the Spirit. How are works of the flesh and the fruits of the Spirit present and active in your life?

Mark 4:13-15

Battling in Intercessory Prayer

READ

Farmers and gardeners know the challenge of improving hardpan, or soil that is compacted. Because hardpan does not have good drainage or enough pore space for roots to expand, it restricts the growth and health of plants.

Paul knew the powers of resistance that come against any attempts to extend the kingdom of God to unbelievers. He advised:

Finally, be strong in the Lord and in the strength of his power. Put on the whole armor of God, so that you may be able to stand against the wiles of the devil. For our struggle is not against enemies of blood and flesh, but against the rulers, against the authorities, against the cosmic powers of this present darkness, against the spiritual forces in the heavenly places (Ephesians 6:10-12).

When we enter into prayer for people who are hard-hearted, those who hear the word but have it quickly stolen from them by Satan, we enter into "spiritual warfare." In the New Testament there is a conflict underway between Jesus (and his disciples) and the spiritual forces that oppose his kingdom. This conflict occurs as a direct result of evangelism efforts that reach out to people who are lost.

Some people within the church are critical of militaristic terms like "spiritual warfare." Yet as a person prays for people to be more receptive to the gospel and stands up for justice, he or she will face opposition, even in the name of Jesus Christ. Conflict is real. The "demonic" takes on human flesh in our very midst. Evil strategies become evident and it is wise to seek the counsel and plan of God to counter these devious plans in a spirit of love and justice. Praying for those who are resistant to the gospel can be a real battle taking a long period of time. God has given you many pieces of armor for your protection in this fight, as well as the sword of the Spirit, which is the offensive weapon of the Word of God. (See Ephesians 6:13-18.)

Jesus expresses a clear concern for those who do not have faith. He also cares deeply for the poor, the marginalized, the oppressed, and others who are pushed to the fringes of society. Utilizing the sword of the Spirit gives God the opportunity to liberate, deliver, heal, and free people who are bound by societal and spiritual bondage. This takes a willingness to obey God, show compassion to the marginalized, and have faith in the power of God. It takes your prayers of intercession as well as your willingness to stand against the powers of evil.

REFLECT

1. Where have you seen evil at work? Have you known anyone who has seemingly been controlled by evil? Does the "spiritual warfare" described in Ephesians 6:10-12 make sense to you? If so, how do you understand it?

2. Which people, groups, or nations is God laying on your heart as an intercessor? Are you willing to keep these in prayer for the long haul? What action is God calling you to take to stand against the forces of opposition?

RESPOND

In *Intercessory Prayer: Praying for Friends and Enemies* (Minneapolis: Augsburg Fortress, 1995), Jane Vennard refers to the "Prayer-Action Cycle." She writes:

> As our commitment to intercession grows, we will discover a congruence in our actions. When we pray for peace, we will act for peace. We might be unable to take specific actions for peacemaking half a world away, but we can translate that distant need into our nearby need and become a peacemaker in our communities, our churches, our families, or our hearts. When we pray for the starving children of the world, we will open our eyes to the physical, emotional, and the spiritual hunger of children closer by and take responsibility for feeding some of those children in some way (p. 29).

How is God leading your prayers into a plan of action? What will you do, where will you do it, and by what date?

Mark 3:1-6

The Religious-Spirited

READ

One of the main ways to open up hardpan soil is to methodically add compost material. Farmers have done this for generations. Plants such as alfalfa and sweet clover are planted in the fall and allowed to grow toward their normal height for a first cutting and then plowed back into the soil. As this plant material is worked in, the soil opens up and allows more room for air. The compost continues to loosen and enrich the soil as it decomposes.

In the Gospel of Mark, the Pharisees and other religious leaders of Jesus' day are representatives of the hard-hearted path in the parable of the sower. They are not only resistant to Jesus' message, they work in opposition to the kingdom of God that Jesus is introducing: "They [the Pharisees] watched him to see whether he would cure him on the sabbath, so that they might accuse him. . . . He [Jesus] looked around at them with anger; he was grieved at their hardness of heart. . . . The Pharisees went out and immediately conspired with the Herodians against him, how to destroy him" (Mark 3:2, 5, 6).

However, Joseph of Arimathea, a member of the Sanhedrin or Jewish council, was a secret follower of Jesus. When the Sanhedrin condemned Jesus and pushed for his death, Joseph did not go along with the plan (Luke 23:51). Joseph loved Jesus so much that he risked his position in the Sanhedrin after Jesus' death by asking for the body so that he could bury it. (See Mark 15:42-46.) This disciple, who was private about his faith throughout Jesus' ministry, turned bold upon his death and provided a tomb that Jesus' own family would not have been able to provide. At the right time, the

Holy Spirit softened Joseph's heart, reducing his fears and moving him to act in faith.

As you pray for those whose hearts seem impossibly resistant to the gospel, remember the slow but effective process of gradually softening hardpan by adding compost material. As with Joseph of Arimathea, God waits and watches for the opportunity to reach the right person at the right time.

REFLECT

Martin Luther pointed out the power of prayer in the life of Augustine, a bishop and theologian in the early church.

> This is what Augustine's mother did. She prayed to God that her son might be converted. But nothing seemed to help. She approached all sorts of learned men and asked them to persuade her son. . . . But when our Lord God came along he acted effectively and made such an Augustine out of him that he's now called an ornament of the church. So James said well, "Pray for one another," etc., for "the prayer of a righteous man has great power in its effects" [James 5:16]. This is one of the best verses in the epistle. Prayer is a powerful thing, if only one believes in it, for God has attached and bound himself to it [by his promises] (*Luther's Works*, vol. 54, Table Talk, edited and translated by Theodore G. Tappert, Philadelphia: Fortress Press, 1967, p. 454).

As you consider praying for hearts that are currently hardpan or resistant to the gospel, reflect on the following prayers of Martin Luther. Pray them and, if you wish, rewrite them for your own use.

1. Dear Lord God, . . . Convert those who are still to be converted that they with us and we with them may hallow and praise thy name, both with true and pure doctrine and with a good and holy life" (Martin Luther, *Luther's Works* [based on the first petition of the Lord's Prayer], vol. 48, Philadelphia: Fortress Press, 1968, p. 195).

2. O dear Lord, God and Father, thou seest how worldly wisdom and reason not only profane thy name and ascribe the honor due to thee to lies and to the devil, but how they also take the power, might, wealth and glory which thou hast given them for ruling the world and thus serving thee, and use it in their own ambition to oppose thy kingdom. . . . Convert those who are still to become children and members of thy kingdom so that they with us and we with them may serve thee in thy kingdom in true faith and unfeigned love (Luther, ibid. [based on the second petition of the Lord's Prayer], p. 195).

3. O dear Lord, God and Father, thou knowest that the world, if it cannot destroy thy name or root out thy kingdom, is busy day and night with wicked tricks and schemes, strange conspiracies and intrigue, huddling together in secret counsel, giving mutual encouragement and support, raging and threatening and going about with every evil intention to destroy thy name, word, kingdom, and children. Therefore, dear Lord, God and Father, convert them and defend us. Convert those who have yet to acknowledge thy good will that they with us and we with them may obey thy will and for thy sake gladly, patiently, and joyously bear every evil, cross, and adversity, and thereby acknowledge, test, and experience thy benign, gracious, and perfect will (Luther, ibid.[based on the third petition of the Lord's Prayer], p. 196).

RESPOND

Write down the names of two or three people who are participating in a congregation. Make a commitment to pray for the opening of these people's hearts to the gospel. Keep this list in front of you for the remainder of this study and record any answers to these prayers.

1. _____

2. _____

3. _____

Family Members

READ

> *Another natural way to loosen compacted soil is with earthworms. Natural agents of aeration, these unseen workers burrow their way through packed soil to consume any decomposing matter and continue the process of softening the soil. Although we cannot see the work being done underground by earthworms, it is a fact that they are a key to healthy soil.*

As you pray for someone who is resistant to the gospel, you are asking the Holy Spirit to work in the life of that person. Although you may not see the results, God is acting upon that individual's life.

Each time that the gospels record Jesus inviting people to follow him, Jesus also speaks of counting the cost of this choice. (See Luke 14:25-33; Mark 8:34-38 and 10:37-38; and Matthew 10:34-39 and 16:24-26.) Jesus has some very difficult words about the priority of following him: "Whoever comes to me and does not hate father and mother, wife and children, brothers and sisters, yes, and even life itself, cannot be my disciple" (Luke 14:26).

When everyone in a family does not believe in, understand, support, or respect the choice to follow Jesus, the cost can include disagreements or tension among family members. Paul's advice to the Corinthians indicates that serious difficulties and challenges also can arise in marrying unbelievers: "Do not be mismatched with unbelievers. For what partnership is there between righteousness and lawlessness? Or what fellowship is there between light and darkness?" (2 Corinthians 6:14).

You may find that members of your family who are unbelievers are more resistant to the gospel than anyone else you know. However, the Bible is filled with stories of people whose lives changed when they encountered Jesus, such as Zacchaeus, the crooked tax collector (Luke 19:1-10), and one of the men crucified with Jesus (Luke 23:40-43).

No heart is too hard for God. We are to pray. It is the Holy Spirit who does the work and "all things can be done for the one who believes" (Mark 9:23).

REFLECT

1. How can the demands and expectations of your family get in the way of being a disciple of Jesus?

2. The most influential people in Timothy's faith development were his grandmother, Lois, and his mother, Eunice (2 Timothy 1:5). Who are the family members or close friends who have been most influential in your faith development?

3. If you are married to an unbeliever, has this raised any problems? If children are involved, how was or is their instruction in Christian faith handled?

RESPOND

Identify a family member who does not believe in Jesus and who you will pray for regularly. How are you already a witness to this person?

Mark 6:1-6

Hometown Friends

READ

Gardeners use broadforks to deal with shallow hardpan in lawns and around flowers and shrubs as well as before planting trees and shrubs. In fact, broadforks may be used once or twice a season simply to break up hardpan and increase aeration.

In Mark 6:1-6, Jesus' efforts to witness and be used by God among hometown friends appear to be fruitless. We too may find that those we want to influence the most with the gospel, those we love as well as those who know us best, are often the most resistant.

If you were part of a non-Christian family and later come to faith in Jesus, this can separate you in many ways from your family. If many of your hometown friends were unbelievers as well, they no longer know how to relate to you when you become a Christian and may even feel threatened by you.

This does not mean that you should simply give up on those you know and love who resist the gospel. The Holy Spirit can transform resistance to powerful faith. This may involve witness and prayer from you, but that doesn't compare to the joy you will experience when a childhood friend comes to faith in Jesus!

Use your intercessory prayers for hometown friends as a gardener would use a broadfork in hardened clay. As you pray, imagine each person's heart as compacted soil in a garden. See God aerating the soil with the broadfork of your prayers so that, in time, when the rain of the Holy Spirit begins to fall, the soil is opened up to receive.

Use your God-given imagination as you pray to see from the present situation to the completion of what you are asking God to accomplish. Be committed to persistent prayer. Jesus' promise to you is this: "Knock, and the door will be opened for you" (Matthew 7:7). Try praying a prayer like the one below:

> Gracious God, Jesus said that he came "to seek and to save the lost." I lift before you my friend (name) and ask that you would open his/her heart to your Holy Spirit. Use me to be a positive witness to (name) that he/she may come to a living faith in you. Jesus, do not allow me to become discouraged but to persist in bringing (name) before you in prayer. I pray this in Jesus' name. Amen

REFLECT

Being a witness to friends from your hometown or friends who aren't part of a congregation can be difficult. You may fear being perceived as pushy or manipulative about your Christian faith. However, if you found a medical doctor you thought was excellent or discovered a reasonably priced restaurant that served excellent food, wouldn't you share that information with your friends? Is there anything that prevents you from having that same desire to share the faith you have in your Lord and Savior?

1. Jesus' birth is announced in Luke 1:26-38. Afterward, Mary left town for more than three months of her pregnancy (Luke 1:39 and 56). What do you think the talk around Nazareth was like during this time?

2. When Jesus began his ministry, the Holy Spirit guided everything he did (Luke 3:21-22; Luke 4:1, 14). This all leads into Jesus' major encounter with his hometown family and friends (Luke 4:16-30). Why do you think the response to Jesus and his teaching changed from kindness (4:22) to rage (4:28-30)?

RESPOND

As we grow in faith, we may see that what we once thought was a coincidence was actually part of an unfolding plan of God. Did God plan where Jesus would be born and grow up? Does God have a plan for you too?

Has God placed people on your path for whom you are to pray and witness? What will you do differently this week as you pray and interact with friends?

Naysayers

READ

A gardener may loosen compacted soil in a garden or flowerbed through a labor-intensive method called double digging. The tools that are required are a spade, a garden fork, and a wheelbarrow. The gardener begins by digging a trench about a foot deep across the width of the garden or bed and putting that topsoil in the wheelbarrow. In the trench, the gardener uses the garden fork to loosen the subsoil, if it isn't too compacted. If it is hardpan, the gardener first breaks up the soil with the spade. The gardener then places the topsoil of the next trench into the trench that was just finished. At the end of the garden, the topsoil in the wheelbarrow is placed into the last trench. The real advantage to double digging is that it loosens the subsoil, which improves aeration and drainage.

Negativity and closed hearts impact the effectiveness of our prayers and make us hesitant to take risks in faith. A labor-intensive method, such as double digging, may be necessary to loosen this compacted soil. Jesus models this for us, in Mark 5, when he "clears the air" to allow a faith-filled atmosphere for healing. Jesus counters an initial wave of naysayers by saying to Jairus, "Do not fear, only believe" (Mark 5:36). When a second wave of naysayers laughs at Jesus' comment that the girl is only asleep, not dead, Jesus puts them outside of the house (5:40).

As a person of prayer, how do you deal with naysayers? If the negative voices are in a prayer group that you participate in, listen first to gain understanding. What is behind the negativity? The people may be in pain because of what they perceive as unanswered prayers.

Second, share with them the promises Jesus makes regarding answers to prayer. Seek to encourage faith. Third, pray for them as well. If all this does not work and negativity persists and begins to affect others in the prayer group, you may need to ask the individuals to step aside from the group. This is admittedly a very difficult step for most people. It is imperative to spend much time prayerfully weighing this situation before you make a decision. Pray that God will keep you and the prayer group humble and repentant as you pray for those who resist the gospel.

REFLECT

1. Members of Jairus's own household told him not to trouble Jesus any further, but Jesus said, "Do not fear, only believe" (Mark 5:35-36). When have you experienced negativity in your life? Perhaps it was when you had a dream, idea, or thought that challenged the status quo. Naysayers can be family members, friends, or simply your own negative thoughts. How do you face negativity?

2. When many naysayers are in positions of power, congregations focus on maintenance rather than their mission. Is your congregation mission-focused or maintenance-driven? What can you do to ensure that your congregation stays clearly focused on mission?

RESPOND

In dealing with naysayers, begin with yourself. Ask the Holy Spirit to prune the dead branches of negativity from your thoughts and life. How will you respond to Jesus' words, "Do not fear, only believe"?

Luke 15:3-7

Praying for the Lost

READ

A gardener can use double digging or a broadfork to loosen and deepen the soil available to plants for healthier produce. The gardener can also loosen and deepen the soil by raising the bed level and increasing the soil depth. To do this, the gardener builds a plank-raised bed and adds topsoil and compost to this new bed, or digs the walkways of the garden down six inches and adds that soil to the bed area. Raised beds yield healthier and more productive plants and flowers because more aerated soil is available to the roots of the plants.

The greatest joy in heaven is when one who is lost is recovered through faith in Jesus. This truth is so important that three parables drive home this point—the parable of the lost sheep (Luke 15:3-7), the parable of the lost coin (Luke 15:8-10), and the story of the son who was lost and comes home to a celebration (Luke 15:11-24). When the lost is found, there is joy in heaven! As we read in 2 Peter 3:9, Jesus came to earth to be the savior of all people: "The Lord is not slow about his promise, as some think of slowness, but is patient with you, not wanting any to perish, but all to come to repentance." The Greek word for "perish, be lost or destroyed" seldom appears in the New Testament. When it does, it is tied to eternal life and the need for repentance (John 3:16; John 10:28; Luke 13:3, 5). God wants no one to be lost.

Our mission remains the same as that of the first disciples. We are to be about the task of making disciples of all people. This can seem overwhelming, but it happens one person at a time. Do not underestimate the power of intercession. The Holy Spirit is the plow that cuts the sod so that the heart can be receptive. At the right time, God will then raise up someone to plant the seed of the gospel in that heart.

REFLECT

Although most mainline congregations do not use language such as "the lost," the term is biblical. For example, Jesus states his purpose in Luke 19:10: "For the Son of Man came to seek out and to save the lost."

1. As intercessors for those who are lost, we are like the four people bringing the man with paralysis to Jesus (Mark 2:1-12). After the four friends take off a roof and let the man down into the home, Jesus says to the man, 'Son, your sins are forgiven" (Mark 2:5). Who are you bringing before Jesus in your prayers?

2. Why was the Ethiopian official ready to receive the witness of Philip (Acts 8:26-40)? Was it a coincidence that Cornelius was prepared to believe the witness of Peter (Acts 10)? The Holy Spirit prepares the hearts of unbelievers to respond in faith to the message of the gospel. This work is done through people who pray and witness. How does this understanding of prayer affect your prayer life?

RESPOND

Commit to praying for the salvation of three or more individuals or families. Place these names on an index card. Write one or two Bible passages on the back side of the card to inspire you to pray for these people. Keep this card in a visible place where you can be reminded to pray frequently, such as in a car, on your bathroom mirror, or at work. What actions will you take a a result of your prayers?

1. _____

2. _____

3. _____

Prayers

- Thomas' travels
- Virginia's Daughter Carol
- Tommy - David & Becky
- Evon Wernthon
- Tim's Sister & Family

Week 4

Praying for the Rocky Ground

Mark 4:5-6

Rocky Ground

READ

Composting is the best way to build up soil because it works with nature's cycle. There are two primary methods of composting. Cold composting is a year-long process of decomposition. Hot composting, which involves more attention and work to maintain the proper moisture and temperature and turn the compost, is the quickest source of fertile compost. The rich nutrients in compost improve the soil's function and make plants more productive.

In the parable of the sower, Jesus refers to "rocky ground." This ground is not like the rich, expansive fields peppered with various sizes of rocks in parts of North America. Instead, it refers to the terraced hillsides of Palestine in Jesus' day. These thin-soiled terraces were cut and leveled out of hills centuries before. Countless trips were made to the valley below to collect soil and haul it back up the hill to level the terraced field and cover the rock shelf where it was bare.

When you begin to pray for new Christians or for those facing hard times, imagine that God is using you to be a laborer carrying compost to cover sprouted seed lying on top of bare rock. You can plead on the behalf of new Christians, that they may see the importance of enriching their spiritual lives by investing themselves in the study of God's word. You can also prayerfully support those entangled in life's problems, that they may see God as a source of strength and hope in the midst of these challenges. These are prayers to help the roots of faith spread and grow.

Rocky ground exists inside as well as outside the church. What is your congregation doing to deepen the soil and help the roots of faith take hold? God created us to live in a faith community. When the body of Christ, the church, functions properly, we are sensitive to the times when another part of the body is at risk and intercede with prayer. However, prayers do not take the place of mentors for new Christians and faith companions for those facing difficulties. Does your congregation have mentors and faith companions for such needs? Perhaps this need could be added to your prayers as well.

REFLECT

The future activity level of visitors, people who are new to the Christian faith, and new members is determined in large part by deep-ened faith lives and involvement in the ministry of the congregation.

1. Using your congregation's membership list, begin to pray for five individuals or families per day. If your congregation is large, this may result in praying for many people you do not know. If your congregation is small, you may want to pray for each group of five for a full week instead of one day. What questions or concerns come to your mind as you spend this time in prayer?

2. As you pray for the members of your congregation, think about how they are involved in the life of your church. Some people were involved just a year ago, but now are not active. Does your congregation provide enough opportunities for every family to be active in some ministry? What can you do to help more members become involved?

3. How does your congregation disciple its adult members? Small groups can assist in this process as people come together to study the Bible, pray, and discuss the challenges of living the Christian life. Do you have a volunteer or paid staff person to coordinate this small group ministry in your congregation? What could be done to enhance your congregation's efforts to make disciples?

RESPOND

Before you pray for others and their discipleship, examine your own life. Are you satisfied with your devotional discipline? What is your daily plan for reading the Bible? How is it going? What is your daily prayer plan? Is there anything that needs to be changed to improve your devotional life? Who holds you accountable to follow your plans or make changes in your devotional life?

Mark 4:16-17

Shallow Soil

READ

In gardening, the best way to combat a shallow soil bed is to add hot compost. This rich and fertile material is developed in a composting bin, where the higher temperatures required for hot composting can be achieved. Hot compost is tilled directly into the soil in the spring and fall and may be added as an organic mulch around plants in the growing season.

In your faith life as a Christian, you start out having very shallow soil. Early on, this may not present problems, but over time you will naturally have questions about your faith. If you do not meet those questions by deepening your faith through reading the Bible, prayer, worship, and Christian fellowship, you are like a sprouting plant in shallow soil. Where there is insufficient soil, your faith cannot spread its roots and is at risk to get scorched, wither, and die when troubles come your way.

Faith-related questions naturally arise as youth differentiate themselves from their parents. Parents who have consistently lived out the Christian faith and Christian peers can provide support and encouragement for faith during this time. Confirmation ministry can also be part of the "composting" process, if it deepens faith development by teaching youth to identify and apply key biblical principles and enter into conversation about faith issues among their peers.

REFLECT

Before you can provide opportunities for new people to grow in Christian faith, you must evaluate the process of deepening faith in your congregation. Focus your prayers on the education and discipleship ministries of your congregation.

1. What plan is in place for the nurture and development of faith of preschoolers in your congregation? How could you advance this ministry?

2. Identify strengths and areas of concern in the deepening of faith and devotional practice of the young people from elementary school through high school. Pray for teachers and youth workers, as well as the children and youth, that their faith may continue to grow and develop. If you choose, talk with the leaders involved with youth and identify ways that you can strengthen this ministry?

3. Talk with those involved in ministries with post-high school young adults, adults, and any small groups about prayer concerns they have for the discipleship of adults in your congregation. What can you do to strengthen this ministry?

RESPOND

Is there any area of discipleship in your congregation that is of special interest to you? Consider how you might become involved. If you are in a prayer group using *Grounded in Prayer*, this week is a good time to talk to your pastor about this study, if he or she is not involved in your group.

WEEK 4 ✦ DAY 3

Mark 8:31-32

Pride

READ

Beginning the composting process in the autumn allows time for material to decompose so that in the spring there is a good source of compost to till into the soil. Leaf mold breaks leaves down and will create a natural compost out of leaves piled together in the fall. In northern areas, gardeners till leaves into garden or flower beds prior to the first snowfall. If the compost material is placed in a garbage can indoors, composting can continue during the winter.

There are many examples of rocky ground in the Gospel of Mark. Mary Ann Tolbert has identified these examples in her book *Sowing the Gospel* (Minneapolis: Fortress Press, 1989, pp. 195-218). She notes that the changing of Simon's name to Peter (which means "rock" in Greek) is a foreshadowing of the disciples as an example of rocky ground.

Like the rocky ground in the parable, the call of the disciples resulted in an "immediate" willingness to follow him (Mark 1:16-20; 2:14). By the middle of the Gospel of Mark, however, the disciples had "hard hearts" and failed to understand what Jesus was all about (8:14-21). When Jesus was arrested, the disciples deserted Jesus. One betrayed him and another denied him (14:10-11, 26-31, 50, 66-72).

According to Proverbs 16:18, "Pride goes before destruction, and a haughty spirit before a fall." In Mark 8, Jesus asks, "Who do you say that I am?" Peter correctly answers, "You are the Messiah" (Mark 8:29). Later on, however, Peter foolishly rebukes Jesus (Mark 8:31-33). Peter became rocky ground, exposing the shallowness of his faith.

Pride is a spiritual danger for us as well. Many congregational splits are the result of a judgmental nature in people who have become involved in prayer. Why does this happen? Our human nature, which is by nature sinful, likes to give voice to how godly we become as we pray and becomes critical of those who are not involved in prayer with us.

The opposite of pride is humility. As Christians, humility is an act of faith in which we acknowledge that God is the creator and that we are part of the creation. As we pray, it is critical to be humble and repentant to keep pride in check. The support of others can help with this.

REFLECT

Pride separates us from God because the focus of pride is on ourselves.

1. Pride is a powerful tool of evil to separate us from God and one another. Recall a time when pride was at work in your life or in the congregation. What was the fruit of that pride? What could have been done to prevent pride from causing separation or division?

2. Jesus said that he had been sent by God to bring salvation to the world so that God would be glorified (John 14:1-14). God wants to be glorified through our lives as well. How can you be humble and also glorify God in your life?

RESPOND

As sure as pride separates us, repentance reunites us! Ask the Holy Spirit to examine your heart, then admit your sin, and repent of it.

What prayer concerns is God bringing to your mind at this moment?

Mark 9:2-13

Fear

READ

The summer months can spell a shortage of needed green material for composting. One of the ways gardeners deal with this is by planting a small crop of additional green plants, such as buckwheat or alfalfa. Before this crop begins to flower, they mow it down, rake the clippings, and add this material to the compost.

In the Bible reading for today, Peter, James, and John have a mountaintop experience with Jesus. They have a miraculous opportunity to be in the presence of the lawgiver, Moses, and the great prophet, Elijah—and to hear the voice of God come out from a cloud. But in the middle of this theophany, or manifestation of God, they are gripped with fear.

The twelve disciples initially responded very positively to the mission of going forth to preach and cast our demons (Mark 3:14-15). In fact, they very successful in carrying out this mission through their teaching and healing ministry (6:7-13, 30). Ironically, they would move from understanding Christ's call to missing the point of it all (compare 4:11-12 with 8:14-21). By the time of Jesus' entry into Jerusalem, the disciples failed to hear and understand Jesus in three sets of passages (8:27—9:29; 9:30—10:31; 10:32-52).

The disciples often were filled with fear. After calming the storm, Jesus rebuked the disciples by asking, "Why are you afraid? Have you still no faith?" (4:40). The disciples were also afraid when Jesus walked on the water (6:47-52) and on the way to Jerusalem (10:32-34).

Fear is a by-product of shallow faith. It is fear that prevents us from praying with confidence and in faith. It is the Word of God that builds trust and enables us to pray with even greater faith. For this reason, it is wise to begin times of prayer and intercession with some reading and reflection on the Bible. God's word gives us confidence to pray in accordance with the promises of God. Fears subside where faith is encouraged and released!

REFLECT

Fears arise when our relationship with God is strained. In John 15:5 Jesus says, "I am the vine and you are the branches." As a branch relies on its connection to the vine for life, we too are to rely on Jesus.

1. Think of a time when you felt very close to God. What were some of the factors that contributed to that sense of closeness? How does this compare with times when you felt distant from God?

2. Very often in biblical stories, when God breaks into the ordinary of life, people of faith are filled with fear. The angel said to Mary, and later to the shepherds, "Do not be afraid" (Luke 1:30; 2:10). How would you feel or how have you felt while experiencing the presence of God?

RESPOND

In John 14:23, Jesus says, "Those who love me will keep my word, and my Father will love them, and we will come to them and make our home with them." Does this passage give you comfort? How will you respond?

Mark 9:33-34

Greatness

READ

A key to successful hot composting is the layering of brown, green, and balanced compost materials. Nitrogen-rich brown materials include straw, hay, leaves, cornstalks, and shredded newspaper. Fresh grass clippings, legume plants, cabbage leaves, and coffee grounds are examples of carbon-rich green compost materials, while balanced materials include fruit peels, vegetables, sod, soil, and garden trimmings. The combination of these ingredients results in the production of fertile compost for a garden.

A balance of repentance, humility, and faith will produce a solid prayer ministry, as well as any other type of ministry. Where these three ingredients for ministry are out of balance, problems begin to surface.

Out of pride, the disciples made comparisons among themselves and asked, "Who among us is the greatest?" Comparing ourselves to others with whom we are in ministry always leads to conflict, as it did for the disciples. When Jesus talked about true greatness, he also gave the disciples an example to follow: "So if I, your Lord and Teacher, have washed your feet, you also ought to wash one another's feet. For I have set you an example, that you also should do as I have done to you. Very truly, I tell you, servants are not greater than their master, nor are messengers greater than the one who sent them" (John 13:14-16).

The greatness that is ours as Christians is found in our relationship with Jesus. Greatness is never about the Christian but about Christ!

REFLECT

These are ripe times for harvesting the hearts of people who are lost into the kingdom of God. It is vital for you to keep a balance of repentance, humility, and faith, which lead to the faithful service of your Lord. Be accountable and wise for the sake of your ministry of prayer.

1. How does the world measure success? Read Luke 14:7-11 and compare the world's values with the kingdom values that Jesus taught in this parable.

2. In Romans 12, Paul gives instructions on how we are to live: "Do not be conformed to this world, but be transformed by the renewing of your minds" (12:2). If we are transformed, how are we different than the world? See Romans 12:3, 9-10.

RESPOND

Have you received answers to prayer? How have you given witness to answered prayers? Think about how you will respond to answered prayers today.

Jealousy

READ

Composting allows a gardener to reduce the amount of garbage by turning yard and garden waste into usable resources. It also enables the gardener to enhance the soil so that plants produce larger and greater amounts of food for consumption.

The disciples showed how shallow their roots of faith were by trying to stop others who were doing ministry in Jesus' name. Jesus rebuked them for that behavior.

There is "thin soil" of faith in our lives too. Today we may criticize other denominations and try to tear them down through our words and actions. Instead, we should thank God that we do not do the work of evangelism and discipleship in our communities alone. Imagine how much work could be done in fulfillment of the Great Commission (Matthew 28:18-20) if we would turn our energies away from criticizing fellow ministers of the gospel to blessing them and praying for their productivity!

We demonstrate our love for God by the way that we love others. People in our communities who do not know the Lord watch the ways congregations behave toward each other. For the sake of our witness and obedience to Christ, we are challenged by these words: "Little children, let us love, not in word or speech, but in truth and action" (1 John 3:18). We have a huge opportunity to pray for sister congregations in the community and denomination. God wants to raise up people who will "stand in the gap" and bless the whole church.

Ask God to fill your heart with the same love that Jesus has for all of his body, the church. If you are in a prayer group, seek ways to connect with similar groups in your community and pray for each other, your witness in your community, and for the love of the Lord to be seen in the ways that you interact and minister together. As we live in the grace that is ours through faith in Jesus, rich compost is added to deepen the soil of faith.

REFLECT

What does the world see if Christians are judgmental and jealous of each other? Are we critical or compassionate in our evaluations of other ministries?

1. Read the parable of the Pharisee and the tax collector in Luke 18:10-14. Do attitudes or prejudices about others come through in your words or actions? Reflect, for example, on your thoughts about people who have less income than you, those in other ethnic groups, and other churches in our own community. Write down a few words of confession.

2. Not one of us is righteous based on how we live our lives, but we are justified before God: "since all have sinned and fall short of the glory of God; they are now justified by his grace as a gift, through the redemption that is in Christ Jesus" (Romans 3:23-24). Write a praise statement to God.

RESPOND

Jesus was clear in teaching about our attitude toward others when he said, "Do not judge, and you will not be judged; do not condemn, and you will not be condemned. Forgive and it will be forgiven" (Luke 6:37). Is there any attitude that you want to release to the Holy Spirit today?

False Authority

READ

The goal of composting is to create healthy plants that yield large produce. Rich and healthy soil results in plants that can sink their roots deep and grow large yields. Adding a foot of fertile compost can cover once rock-bare surface and produce deep-rooted plants.

In Mark 10:13-16, Jesus' disciples misunderstand the importance of reaching out to all people, regardless of age. Jesus makes it clear that we enter the kingdom of God by embracing the gospel with trusting faith, like that of a child.

Baptism has been an entry point for people into the community of faith. Baptism is also a re-entry point for couples returning to the church with a child to be baptized. Baptisms provide opportunities to reconnect young families to faith in Christ and to the community of faith.

In many congregations, an outreach-based vacation Bible school is another entry point. This is an opportunity to introduce children to a living faith in Jesus and follow up with other ministries for parents. Sunday school may be the next step. Parenting or budgeting classes may be other steps.

The rocky ground in the parable of the sower refers not only to those who have fallen away from the church but may represent people who are at risk to fall away in the future because they do not have deep lives of faith. Bible study, prayer groups, and other activities that include Christian fellowship can help the roots of faith to sink deeper into people's lives.

REFLECT

The mission for all Christian congregations of the church is the same—to make disciples of all people (Matthew 28:18-20). What is unique to each congregation is the vision for ministry that God has for each one. Prayer enables the congregation to move beyond its own best understanding and evaluation of the situation to receive God's vision.

1. When the Jews found themselves with nowhere else to turn for help, God sent the prophet Jeremiah to announce a message of hope. When your congregation finds itself in desperate times, there is reason to hope in God as well. Jesus, the head of the church, cares more about your congregation than you do. As you pray and wait for God's vision, meditate on these words of hope: "Call to me and I will answer you, and will tell you great and hidden things that you have not known" (Jeremiah 33:3). What is God saying to your congregation?

2. In John 14-16, Jesus outlines three principles of prayer: asking in Jesus' name, in accordance with his will, and for the glory of God (John 14:13-14; 15:16; 16:23-26). Write a prayer for the rocky ground in the hearts of people in your congregation and community.

RESPOND

As you prayerfully seek and consider God's vision for you and your congregation, what is God showing you? What will you do with this vision?

Week 5

Praying for the Thorny Ground

Mark 4:7, 18-19

Thorny Ground

READ

There are more than 100 plants in Palestine that fall into the category often translated as thorns or thistles. The most common plant is called Scolymus: "This is a noxious weed abundant in the grain fields. It is three to four feet high. The stem is provided with spiny wings, and its green leaves have white patches and veins. The yellow flowers are arranged in spiny heads. On fallow ground it occupies large stretches" (M. Zohary, *The Interpreter's Dictionary of the Bible*, vol. 2, Nashville: Abingdon Press, 1962, p. 297).

The United States does not seem to have an equivalent to this nasty weed, which sounds like a cross between a Canadian thistle and a bramble plant. New shoots of the Scolymus plant grow in tight proximity to each other, like a patch of thistles. Similar to a thistle, you can hoe this weed down but since the source of life is found in its roots it quickly sends up new shoots. It outdistances domestic grains like wheat or barley in its growth patterns and effectively chokes these grains out.

Isaiah may have been referring to this plant in his condemnation of all the enemies of Judah: "Thorns shall grow over its strongholds, nettles and thistles in its fortresses" (Isaiah 34:13). This same plant is referred to in Job 31:40, and a close relative is mentioned in the curse of the ground by God in the Garden of Eden story: "cursed is the ground because of you; in toil you shall eat of it all the days of your life; thorns and thistles it shall bring forth for you" (Genesis 3:17-18).

In today's Bible reading, the sower continues to broadcast the precious seed, even in the areas of the field where it is at risk of being overcome by thorns. This is not an account of a foolish farmer. On the contrary, this sower is so filled with grace that he casts the seed into the soil even where its survival is highly at risk.

As Christians, we are aware that there are many thorns in our world that work to choke out the seeds of faith. We have seen many eager people come into the church only to disappear because the lure and demands of the world have choked out the seed of faith. The thorny ground knows no limits and chokes out the faith of new as well as long-standing Christians.

Our prayers must be directed at the heart of the church, that the seed may be planted deep within it. Also, pray that we may be so committed to each other that we can count on the prayers and encouragement of our Christian brothers and sisters for needed support.

REFLECT

In *Mere Christianity*, C. S. Lewis wrote, "If I find in myself a desire which no experience in this world can satisfy, the most probable explanation is that I was made for another world. If none of my earthly pleasures satisfy it, which does not prove that the universe is a fraud. Probably earthly pleasures were never meant to satisfy it, but only to arouse it, to suggest the real thing" (New York: MacMillan, 1960, p. 106).

1. Many congregations have come to see the great value in praying regularly for their membership. Who can you invite to join you in gathering each week to pray for your members? When will you begin this new ministry? Invite and inform your pastor of your intentions. Communicate with the congregation and encourage anyone who is interested to join you in this ministry of prayer.

2. Other targets for prayer are visitors in worship and all new members. One way to pray for visitors by name is to have people write their names and other information on worship or friendship pads during worship services. Some of these forms include space for prayer concerns. Many congregations send members out on short home visits to thank visitors for worshiping and leave a plate of cookies or a loaf of freshly baked bread. In addition to this contact, a note from a prayer group that informs visitors that prayers have been said for them can be a word of care. It is also effective to pray and send a note to new members. A prayer request form can be included in this type of note. Would such a prayer ministry interest you or others in your congregation?

RESPOND

As ideas for prayer expand within your congregation, you may want to look for a volunteer or part-time staff person to coordinate this ministry. Can you think of people who might feel called to develop an intentional prayer ministry?

Mark 10:17-27

Wealth and Possessions

READ

What makes a plant a weed is that it is located in the wrong place.
Some look like the grains or grasses that they grow alongside, while
others weeds have a poisonous or spiny exterior. Some have a nasty
underground creeping root system for germinating new plants.
Others have a taproot that runs deep underground and sends up
new shoots.

At the very least, the thorny ground that Jesus referred to in the
parable of the sower was protected by some pernicious, perennial
weeds that likely had a taproot. When the farmer would attempt to
root out these weeds, he first had to pay the price of venturing into
the patch. Second, there was the hard work of hoeing or cutting the
weeds down. Next came the challenge of digging up the root system
to slow down future new starts. Finally, there would be latent seeds
laying in the soil, which may have numbered in the tens of thousands
per plant.

In Mark's Gospel, the story of the rich man serves as an example
of thorny ground, the third type of soil in the parable of the sower.
The rich man's spiritual quest was similar to the journey of all who
seek to understand life from a perspective of faith: "What must I do
to inherit eternal life?" (verse 17). This man's overall sin has tradition-
ally been interpreted as being pride. If this is the case, why did Jesus
love him? As Eduard Schweizer points out, "For centuries [this] question had been asked by those who came to the temple in Israel, and
the priests reminded them of the commandments, as Jesus does here"
(*The Good News According to Mark*, Atlanta: John Knox Press, 1977,
p. 210).

What is of greatest significance in this story is the repeated call of Jesus to discipleship. This call is universal, meaning that it is for everyone. However, the action taken is unique to each personal situation. At its center, discipleship is the yielding of one's life to Jesus alone as Lord. Because we cannot serve two or more "lords" in our lives, Jesus' call to follow him demands sole allegiance (Matthew 6:24). For some, this means leaving fishing boats or tax offices. For the rich man, it meant selling his possessions and giving the wealth away to the poor. For others, it means remaining in their communities as living witnesses to Jesus (Mark 5:19).

As we search out the thorns in our own hearts and name those distractions that clamor for attention, we are better prepared to pray for the thorny ground and for those who battle with the choking cares of the world.

REFLECT

The lure of wealth is very powerful. Television has caught this wave and moved from game shows that give away thousands of dollars to the chance to be a millionaire. Bumper stickers announce all types of slogans about wealth, such as "The one who dies with the most toys, wins."

1. Read and reflect on Philippians 4:10-13. How do you differentiate between wants and needs in your life? Have you quenched the appetite for more wealth in your life? Have you learned to be content with what you have been entrusted with in this life?

2. What do you think Jesus meant when he said the following? "Children, how hard it is to enter the kingdom of God! It is easier for a camel to go through the eye of a needle than for a rich man to enter the kingdom of God" (10:24-25). As you pray for those who are distracted by wealth, remember what Jesus said when the disciples asked about who can be saved: "With mortals this is impossible, but not for God; for God all things are possible" (10:27).

RESPOND

Jesus said that "the cares of the world, and the lure of wealth and the desire for other things come in and choke the word, and it yields nothing" (Mark 4:19). Write a prayer for people caught in the powerful grip of wealth, naming that power and asking for release from its grip, in Jesus' name. Visualize greed as a strong weed that you are pleading with God to uproot. Ask God to uproot this weed in your life and show you ways to help and encourage others dealing with it.

Family Members

READ

> *Weeds have been a part of our human struggle since ancient times. Farmers and gardeners alike know the annual war that they must wage against the determination of weeds. From chemical warfare, to cultivation and the use of mulch, no approach has eliminated the continued existence of this nuisance. Weeds continue to live on and to be a thorn in the side of those who work the soil.*

Jesus' words about hating our family members are very strong. Families can demand our full devotion, but Jesus' words make the point that even our closest blood relatives cannot stand in the way if we want to be his disciples. This is a decisive call that Jesus gives to us. By using the strong word *hate*, Jesus is driving a wedge into our hearts so we must choose whom we will serve with total devotion.

When a lawyer approached Jesus and asked the same question that the rich man asked about eternal life, Jesus asked him what the law said. He answered, "You shall love the Lord your God with all of your heart, and with all of your soul, and with all of your strength, and with all of your mind; and your neighbor as yourself" (Luke 10:27). We are to love God with our whole being, and love ourselves and our neighbor. Properly understood, we begin by loving God. Jesus did not intend to suggest that we are to hate anyone. God is about love. Where our primary devotion lies is what matters, and it must lie with God.

Faith in Jesus is a costly decision in many non-Christian nations. Christians in parts of Asia or some Islamic nations knows that this faith decision will mean losing their family because they will be removed as family members. In these places, Christian faith can also mean job loss, other hardships, and even death.

Faith in Jesus can also be costly in the United States, especially for those who come to faith in Jesus as Lord from a non-believing or non-Christian family. Family systems can be threatened by a member who becomes a Christian. Demeaning jokes and harsh remarks can be commonplace. The apostle Paul recognized the difficulties that exist when a Christian marries a non-Christian. How does a Christian pray for and witness to a non-Christian spouse?

In Week 3, Day 4, we looked at the hard-heartedness that you may find in members of your family. As you seek to be an effective witness, interceding for your family members who don't believe in Jesus may be the most difficult praying you do. Ask God to raise up witnesses for your family members so that they may come to a living faith in Christ. Name the other "lords" that presently stand in the way of faith for them. Imagine these other gods being weeded out of their hearts. Persist in your prayers until your family members have come to faith in Jesus.

REFLECT

Many powers are at work to try to prevent us from yielding our lives to God. Even those who are closest to us can be a deterrent to our faith.

1. God is graciously committed to a relationship with you. Paul writes, "For I am convinced that neither death, nor life, nor angels, nor rulers, nor things present, nor things to come, nor powers, nor height, nor depth, nor anything else in all creation, will be able to separate us from the love of God in Christ Jesus our Lord" (Romans 8:38-39). As you think about God's incredible commitment to this relationship with you, write a response of thanksgiving to God.

2. Praying for the salvation of family members is one of our most important intercessions. It can also be very difficult if pain is associated with memories of your family. Even Jesus had family members—brothers—who did not believe in him (John 7:5). Keep a picture of your family members close at hand so that you can remember to pray for them each day.

RESPOND

Are you willing to commit to pray for an open heart to the gospel for members of your family who do not attend church? Praying with a prayer partner about these concerns may make it easier for you. Ask God to lead you in these prayers.

Mark 5:1-2, 11-17

Career Success

READ

Organic mulch can keep weeds from germinating in walkways and around plants. Organic mulch works by blocking sunlight from the weeds. It can include dry leaves, hay, lawn clippings, cardboard or newspaper. The hay or straw must be as free of weed seed as possible. Enough sheets of newspaper need to used so that when the paper gets wet, weeds will not simply break through.

The hog farmers in the nation of the Gerasenes were eager to have Jesus leave town! They had lost all of their boss's investment and may have been in danger of losing their jobs as a result. How could they ever explain what had just taken place?

Work and careers are important parts of life. One of the first questions we ask each other while getting acquainted is, "What do you do for a living?" Somehow our work defines something about who we are. But is that really true? We certainly invest a good amount of our most productive time at the workplace. Studies show that Americans are working more hours today than ever. If we work nine to 10 hours a day, commute one to two hours to work each day, and sleep seven hours a night, we are left with five to seven hours of time awake at home.

There are many issues here that require prayer. When work begins to rob people of healthy family relationships, personal well-being, and growth opportunities for faith, it is functioning as a weed, choking out the purpose of life as God intended it.

Do you live to work or work to live? If you are employed, you may see your job as important to society. If so, this is a gift. Work may also give you a sense of accomplishment or fulfillment as a person.

However, in a society that values work so much, there is a temptation to become a slave to your work and make your work into a god.

Many people need to work more than one job to make a living. This can be demanding on the individual, to say nothing of the impact it has on relationships and families. It also makes it more challenging for people to worship, grow in faith through involvement in a small group Bible study or prayer group, or participate in some other aspect of servant ministry. Faith can really suffer as a result of work!

REFLECT

Issues related to work are very significant for your life, health, and faith. Use the following questions as a starting point for your thoughts and reflection.

1. If you are employed, how do you define success in relation to your work? What is the cost of success in your work? Who is positively and negatively impacted by your success? If you could change one or two things about your work, what would they be? Is there a change that would improve your life, health or faith?

2. Think about people (perhaps this includes you) who need to work two or three jobs to stay financially afloat. What types of support can your congregation provide for these individuals and families? Perhaps the congregation could provide a forum for discussion on the nature of work and its challenges today or a place for people to share concerns and build networks with each other.

RESPOND

Write a prayer that embraces the needs of people who are employed, unemployed, underemployed, underpaid, or over-committed to work and success.

Mark 1:35-39

Over-Committed

READ

Plastic mulch works well to prevent weeds, although it does not allow moisture to seep through into the soil or feed soil like organic mulch. Black plastic heats up the soil as it attracts the sun's rays, which is good for some plants but not for others.

Jesus was fully human and had to make choices regarding his time and his life. In today's Bible reading, Jesus pauses to find solitude for prayer, meditation, and reflection before going out to minister throughout Galilee. We too need to take time for prayer, meditation, and reflection. The demands of life can be great. It takes discipline to remain focused on the things that matter most for spiritual, physical, and relational health. Without this discipline, you may function well for a time, but at some point your health and faith will suffer. Even the need to intercede for others in prayer can get out of balance in our lives. When this happens, you need to step back, reevaluate, and make some changes to recapture your focus.

What are some indicators that your life is out of balance? Consider these:

✦ Your attitude is negative in many areas of your life.

✦ You have become judgmental of family members or others close to you.

✦ Your energy level has diminished, leaving you exhausted.

✦ You have become a poor listener and turn conversations toward yourself.

✦ You complain frequently about almost anything.

- Your devotional time has dried up or you ignore it altogether.
- Nothing seems to relax you.

At times when your life is out of balance, how can you regain your focus and restore health? The first step is to evaluate your life and prioritize your commitments. If your perspective is skewed because your life is so out of balance, ask a trusted friend to help you prioritize the parts of your life. The lure of the things of the world is real to all of us. Sometimes we allow other people's expectations or demands to control us. Or we try to live at an economic level that we cannot sustain in a healthy way. In what ways could you simplify your life? Inner peace and health are more valuable and lasting than appearances.

Additionally, restore personal discipline, especially in the areas of exercise, healthy eating, devotional and prayer life, and rest. Do not skip this step! Rest can turn your health and attitude around quickly and is as key to your health as a tune-up is to a misfiring car engine. Lastly, push back obligations that are not important and eliminate what is not essential to you.

As you examine your own struggles with priorities and discipline, you will find ways to pray for those whose relationships and faith are being torn by life's demands.

REFLECT

Everything you do may be important, but not at the expense of health and faith. If you over-commit and find yourself rushing everywhere you go, life quickly loses its luster. Many people get caught in this trap.

1. If you or someone close to you is suffering from over-commit-ment, what would need to change if you, or that person, were sick and homebound for three months? How would you reorganize and delegate your work and other commitments? What changes can you make right now to simplify your life? If appropriate, identify people to mentor or train to handle some of your com-mitments, responsibilities or projects.

2. How does your congregation encourage healthy living? Is there a system in place in your congregation to prevent over-commitment to the ministries of the church? If not, what can be done to change that?

RESPOND

What are your top five priorities in life? Examine the amount of time you invest in each of these areas. Does the percentage and the quality of the time you invest reflect your priorities? If it does, praise God! If it does not, how will you reorganize your time? Ask for God's guidance in this process.

Mark 10:28-31

Power

READ

When farmers plant a crop like soybeans in a tight pattern and the beans begin to shade the soil, excellent living mulch is produced. Living mulch is able to crowd out some types of weeds organically.

Issues of power can crowd out faith in our lives. Power, or the ability to influence and control situations, takes many shapes. The first type of power in our society is held by those with wealth. Material resources determine many policies and give instant access to those who are rich.

Second, there are positions of power within organizations and communities that greatly influence the climate and decisions. The mayor, police chief, fire chiefs, council members, the president of the chamber of commerce, union leaders, the superintendent of schools, and bank presidents are examples of power positions within a community. When healthy servants lead a community, community life is good. But when corruption infects the leaders, it impacts the whole community.

A third type of power may be termed "corporate power." This is potentially one of the most evil and destructive forms of power. Profit is the god that drives much of the corporate world. Huge networks of dominant corporations have strongholds in countless nations. Corporations that abuse power can and have held nations hostage due to their debt, providing income only to a few. Life can be good for many in this system but historically the environment, people's health, and other nations have suffered due to this system.

A fourth type of power is national or super-power status given to a few dominant nations, including the United States. From the perspective of the United States, many other nations have been supported and strengthened by our "Big Brother" role in the world. However, the United States and other super-power nations have also inflicted pain on many innocent people in the world.

A fifth type of power is spiritual power. The Bible talks about a dualism of power: the power of light and the power of darkness. There is a destructive spiritual force at work that is consuming many lives, often times women and children. This is the reality of evil. There are spiritual roots behind many oppressive patterns, such as alcoholism, drug abuse, physical violence, incest, and rape.

Even greater than all of the forces of evil is the power of God at work in each one of us. The Bible says, "the one who is in you is greater than the one who is in the world" (1 John 4:4). Jesus gave his disciples power and authority over evil as they were sent out to extend the kingdom of God through preaching and healing (Luke 9:1-2).

Christ has won the ultimate victory (Colossians 2:15). With this confidence that is ours in Christ Jesus, we enter into prayer.

REFLECT

All power ultimately comes from God but much power on earth is distorted and twisted for human gain. When Pilate was questioning Jesus prior to his crucifixion, he alluded to his power to free or condemn Jesus: "Jesus answered him, 'You would have no power over me unless it had been given you from above'" (John 19:11).

1. Read 1 Timothy 6:6-10. Reflect on how money has power for good and the power to cause division in your personal life and in the congregation.

2. Jesus was often in conflict with the religious authorities of his day over the interpretation of God's law. This was a struggle over power and control. How is this experienced in the church today? Around which issues might Jesus disagree with the leaders of the church? Prayerfully consider what changes may need to occur for the church to carry out its mission.

RESPOND

According to 1 Timothy 2:1-4, we are to pray for the people in positions of power. It is not difficult to pray for people you have helped to elect into office. How will you keep other leaders and global leaders in your prayers? (For example, the leaders of Israel and the Palestinians.) What is God burdening your heart to pray for regarding the various powers in this world? Is there any action you will take as a result of these prayers?

John 8:3-11

Inability to Let Go of the Past

READ

Sometimes there is nothing else to do but roll up your sleeves and get to work. When all else fails, gardeners deal with weeds head on through the hard work of the hoe.

The fears and pain of yesterday hold many people back from facing today and tomorrow with hope. The grasp of the past has amazing strength as it chokes out the joy of the present. Its grip is tenacious as it repeatedly reminds an individual that he or she is its captive, snagged by the pains of the past. The result is an underlying misery.

How can the mistakes and hurts of yesterday have so much power today? One way is through your reputation. Other people can serve to remind of you of things that occurred long ago, sometimes even delighting in the retelling. In order to start over and establish a new reputation, some people avoid class reunions or move to a new community.

Another way that the past haunts us is by making us unable to receive the forgiveness of God. Guilt or shame can have such a strong grasp on us that we do not think it is possible for God to ever forgive us. The Bible is clear that there is forgiveness available for all sin through the Lord Jesus Christ: "If we confess our sins, he who is faithful and just will forgive us our sins and cleanse us from all unrighteousness" (1 John 1:9). A person who is a victim of molestation, rape, or abuse may need help in overcoming the past. In addition to therapy, prayers for release from guilt and shame may be needed.

It is one thing to receive God's forgiveness, but it is another to forgive yourself. This is a second step in the process of receiving healing from past hurts. In some cases, work with a therapist or counselor may be needed to realize that you are gaining nothing by holding onto your pain.

It is yet again an entirely different issue to forgive the one who has hurt you. Though it seems justifiable to hold unto this anger or bitterness, who is really hurt when you retain these negative emotions? It is God's place to judge, so it is wise to let go, forgive, and release the other person into God's hands. This enables you to finally be set free from the hurts of the past.

You do not need to be bound to the past. Painful memories from the past can be healed and your hope can be restored as you receive healing for yesterday's hurts. Work with a therapist, counselor, spiritual director or pastor may prove helpful. Sometimes it takes a combination of people to support you through this process. Do not be surprised that it takes time to receive inner healing. It is well worth the work, time, and money to receive the freedom to face the future with hope.

REFLECT

In the Bible reading for today, a woman is brought before Jesus because she had been caught in the act of adultery. The religious leaders watch to see how Jesus will react. In keeping with the laws of Leviticus, the men were ready to stone this woman. Imagine the fear the woman experienced.

1. Has there ever been a time when you found it difficult to believe that God would forgive you? When was that time, and what enabled you to receive God's forgiveness?

2. Is there anything for which you have not forgiven yourself? What is holding you back from doing this?

3. Is there anyone you have not forgiven? Who is getting hurt by this? Are you willing to forgive that person right now?

RESPOND

People invariably get hurt within congregations because it consists of sinful human beings. How has your congregation dealt with those hurts in terms of confession and forgiveness in the past? How might God be calling your congregation to deal with hurts in the future? Are there hurts that need to be confessed, even now?

Week 6

Blessing the Good Soil

Good Soil

READ

Plants produce better when they grow alongside members of the same family rather than next to adversarial plants. A gardener takes this into account when planning a garden. For example, broccoli, Brussels sprouts, cauliflower, cabbage, kale, kohlrabi, radishes, and turnips, which are all in the cabbage family, are planted next to each other. They are not placed alongside their adversarial plants, such as strawberries and pole, snap, and lima beans.

As important as planning is for maximum productivity from a garden, it is even more important for a congregation to have a holistic plan for evangelism through discipleship and incorporation. The old model of moving visitors into membership has failed in many cases because it did not take into consideration the spiritual, social, and ministry needs of individuals and families. Rather, it often focused on how new people could fit into an existing structure to further existing organizational goals. How does this compare with how membership is understood in your congregation?

People come to congregations because of an interest and need in their lives. Generally, they are looking for two things: assistance in finding God and ways to meet relationship or friendship needs. Getting to know these individuals, listening to their questions and reasons for coming, and serving them as well as we can takes a discipleship plan that is flexible enough to meet their needs.

In addition to greeters who welcome all people who come to worship, some congregations have added "ambassadors" who are trained to serve the needs of newcomers. This ministry may include welcoming newcomers, showing them to the nursery and introducing them to the caregivers, bringing them to the appropriate Sunday school classrooms and introducing them to teachers, inviting them to worship, and assisting with any questions. Ambassadors may give newcomers their phone numbers in case other questions arise.

Once an ambassador has connected with an individual or family, he or she stays in contact until newcomers complete an introductory class. This class often addresses the issues of becoming a Christian, the ministry of the congregation, membership and what that may mean, additional classes, and a covenant of commitment to Christ and his church. Until the newcomers are ready to attend this class, ambassadors send them thank-you notes and follow up with friendly phone calls to answer questions and encourage them to return to worship.

REFLECT

Ministry to people who are seeking God or a church is primarily one of service, but it has evangelism at its core. It is a ministry focused on how we can serve the newcomer, in the belief that the day will come when the invitation to believe and follow Jesus will be accepted. It is all about God's timing. There is a shift in thought, from having newcomers become members and help the congregation, to discipleship. The question for each newcomer is: How can we assist you in discerning your gifts and calling as you continue to grow in what it means to be a follower of Jesus? Ministries that have never been done in the congregation before may be what a newcomer feels called to do. That's exciting!

1. Read and ponder Mark 1:35-39. Jesus had his prayer time interrupted by his disciples who were overwhelmed by all the people searching for him. Note how Jesus responds. What did Jesus say he had come to do?

2. Good soil is good because it is receptive to the seed, which is the Word of God. It begins to grow in faith in Jesus as Lord. Pray for receptivity to the preaching and the teaching of God's word that takes place at your congregation. How can your congregation pray for this more intentionally?

RESPOND

How is God moving you to respond on behalf of newcomers seeking God? Could there be seekers in your Sunday school and confirmation ministry?

In some congregations, individuals come to the church before worship services to pray that those at worship will be receptive to the gospel message. Some individuals pray for Sunday school teachers and students as well. Consider doing this as an individual, family, or prayer group. You may want to invite others in the congregation to join you.

Mark 5:1-20

The Marginalized

READ

Each family of plants has a different impact on the soil, so it is wise to rotate plant families from year to year in different areas of the garden. For example, if the bean family, which puts nitrogen back into the soil, is followed by sweet corn, which relies on that nitrogen, the result is better corn yields. One year a gardener may plant sweet corn in the northwest corner of the garden, alongside the cucumber family, with the bean family in the northeast corner. In the southern half of the garden the gardener may plant the carrot family, the cabbage family, and the tomato family. The following year, the plan may be to rotate the order in the north and in the south. In year three, the plan may be to flip-flop the plants that are in the north and south.

The Gospel of Mark offers many examples of good soil. One example is the demon-crazed man, who had broken free from the shackles and chains used to restrain him and was now in Jesus' face. But seeing the receptive soil in this man takes real discernment. The story takes place not in a Jewish area but in the nation of the Gerasenes, part of the Decapolis region that was a league of 10 primarily Gentile towns established after the Roman conquest.

The community had unsuccessfully attempted to restrain the man on the edge of town in the cemetery. According to Jewish beliefs, an individual living among the dead would be seen as profane or unclean. The hog farmers and 2,000 drowned hogs would be considered unclean as well. In addition, there is a spiritual confrontation between Jesus and the man and his demons. In spite of all this, Jesus looked beyond how the man was dressed, his homelessness, and even his crazed behavior. Jesus could see what this man could become when freed from spiritual and social bondage.

Many people in our communities live on the edges of society due to the control and economics of those in power. In the case of the Gerasene demoniac, a spiritual possession caused bizarre behavior, which resulted in his expulsion from the community. Today we have distanced ourselves from this spiritual reality so that we rarely discuss the power of Satan and are ill-prepared to minister for release and deliverance as Jesus did in this story. Although Satan must not become the focus of our discussion or prayers, we would be unwise to ignore the spiritual reality described in the New Testament, especially in Ephesians 6.

Jesus came to set captives free. He also challenged the value systems that we use to screen who we think we should evangelize. Jesus looked beyond outward appearances into the soil of the heart. May we have the courage to pray through our biases and prejudices and seek the compassionate heart of Jesus, who desires all to be saved—especially those pushed to the edge of our communities.

REFLECT

Every community has people who live on the periphery and experience rejection and isolation as a result. Congregations can build bridges to these people and demonstrate love and community.

1. As you reflect on the story from Mark 5:1-20, how do you think the demoniac felt when he saw Jesus coming near him? Living in the cemetery, do you think he had heard about Jesus and his ministry?

2. Read Isaiah 61:1-4. Jesus read this text in the synagogue in his hometown of Nazareth. Afterward, Jesus said, "Today this scripture has been fulfilled in your hearing" (Luke 4:21). What do you think Jesus meant by that statement? Make a list of the ministries that are being referred to in Isaiah 61. How is your congregation currently engaged in some of these or other caring ministries? Praise God for those ministries today. What plan may God have for your congregation to further advance this care for others?

RESPOND

To carry out a ministry to people who are marginalized will take at least a small group of committed and passionate people. Identify some people who might participate in this kind of ministry with you.

Mark 5:21-24a, 35-43

Religious Leaders

READ

The growing season and soil temperature of any garden is important in determining what you plant, how you plant, and when you plant. Gardeners must know the growing season and soil temperature for the area and then read seed packets carefully. Rapidly changes in weather can spell disaster for plants. Unexpected frost can be a real killer, causing people to work at a fevered pitch in places, such as the Florida orange groves.

Driven by desperation, Jairus, a synagogue leader, sought out Jesus for a miracle of healing for his dangerously ill daughter. Jairus fell at Jesus' feet and begged him to come and lay his hands on the girl, believing that this would save her life. His need for the Lord provides a receptive heart to the person and message of Jesus. Jairus was good soil!

The experience of Jairus demonstrates that not all religious leaders were disinterested in Jesus. Many people in the church today are quick to verbally attack their pastors and other leaders. Imagine how different things would be if there was a team of people in each congregation praying with and for the leaders of the church each week.

REFLECT

Jesus is the head of the church, which is the body of Christ (Ephesians 4:14-16). Because God is a God of order and not chaos, the church is organized with appointed leaders to guide, spiritually build up, and equip the whole congregation for various ministries both within the church and in the community (Ephesians 4:12).

1. Jesus needed and sought the prayers of his disciples in his darkest hours in the garden of Gethsemane. (Read Mark 14:32-42.) When have you benefited from the prayers of others? Can you think of a time that you wished you had someone praying for you?

2. The apostle Paul saw his need to rise up in prayer for the sake of his ministry (Ephesians 6:19-20; Colossians 4:3-4; 1 Thessalonians 5:25; and 2 Thessalonians 3:1-2). How does your congregation intentionally pray for your pastor(s)? Do you pray for your congregational leaders in any strategic way? How may God be leading you to pray with and for them?

RESPOND

If there are no intentional prayers for your congregational leaders and pastor(s) at this time, consider starting such a ministry. How could you invite others to participate in this?

Mark 5:25-34

The Chronically and Terminally Ill

READ

Three basic ingredients needed for healthy plants are nutrient-rich soil, adequate sunlight, and sufficient moisture. For sufficient moisture, a gardener can supplement natural rainfall with irrigation or watering. Using mulch around the plants also helps by conserving moisture until there is some natural shading from the growth of the plants themselves.

A person's name is a basic part of his or her identity. Yet in yesterday's Bible reading, Jairus's daughter is restored to life but we do not learn her name.

Today's reading contains another example of a significant encounter between Jesus and a woman who unfortunately goes unnamed. This woman had hemorrhaged for 12 years and had spent all her money on doctors with no relief. According to the purification laws of the Jews, she was ritually unclean—and, consequently, she was making anyone in the crowd who touched her unclean as well (Leviticus 15:25-33). Likewise, she made Jesus ritually unclean by touching his garment. Encountering people who were considered unclean never stopped Jesus from healing, however. In some instances, Jesus became ritually unclean himself by touching a leper (Mark 1:40-42).

Like Jairus, this woman was desperate. She was also willing to break the purification laws out of a need and desire to be healed. The woman was receptive soil for the gospel as she weaved her way through the crowd to Jesus. "If I but touch his clothes, I will be made well" (Mark 5:28), she said. She was like a dry sponge soaking up the living water, which was Jesus' presence. The chronically ill woman was healed.

Many people today battle long-term or terminal illnesses, either their own illnesses or that of a family member. These illnesses often affect families by consuming members of the household with a whole new lifestyle and focus. Days melt into months of time spent in and out of hospitals. Meals are sporadic and rushed, sleep is irregular, and exercise is rare. Life is turned upside down for all of those fighting long-term and terminal illnesses. Any connections to a congregation are sometimes lost.

In spite of this, we see in the woman's story in Mark 5 that there is a hunger for hope and healing as people live in desperation. As we pray for others, this is a field ready for harvest. We need to pray for God to raise up laborers to accompany a person who is ill and the family. Second, we can intercede for people who are ill and their family members by name, asking for seeds of the hope we have in Jesus to be planted deep in good and receptive soil in these hearts.

REFLECT

Jesus spent a great portion of his ministry healing those who were sick. He did not shy away from people who were ill but was willing to risk breaking the rules to touch and heal them. Jesus also said that when we care for the sick, we care for him (Matthew 25:31-40).

1. Read James 5:14-16. James encourages us to offer prayers for those who are sick. Does your congregation offer services of healing or anointing? Have you ever experienced healing in your life? Has anyone you prayed for had his health improve or her healing under doctors' care occur more rapidly than expected? Was there a miraculous healing?

2. Some people feel disconnected to God and the church because of "unanswered prayer." Others have lost confidence in God after praying for loved ones only to have them die. What have you experienced with prayers for loved ones or others who are terminally ill? Listen in prayer to what God may be showing you.

3. As believers in Christ, we hold to the reality that death is not the end but rather the beginning. Some congregations have ministers who are trained to do caring visitation at hospitals and homes. Hospice can be another effective ministry of compassion and care. How can your congregation develop or enhance a ministry of care and support for those dealing with terminal illnesses?

RESPOND

As you pray, are there any new directions that you receive from God for your congregation? There are many families who go through the pain of the death of a loved one without faith in Jesus. As they look for hope and something to hold onto, these people can be receptive soil for the gospel. What is God calling you to do?

Mark 7:24-30

Outsiders

READ

*In the northern half of the United States, gardeners start many
plants indoors because of the short growing season. Transplanting
the seedlings, like planting seed, works best if there is abundant
water and warm and loosened soil. A gardener must handle
seedlings carefully during transplanting to prevent damage to the
roots or leaves. Because newly transplanted seedlings are so fragile,
the gardener initially covers them at night to provide protection
from wind and sun while the plants set root.*

Transplanting can be a helpful metaphor as we give thought to
the good and receptive soil of "outsiders." For this discussion, an
"outsider" is any individual or group not currently included in the
life of the congregation. This can be a substantial group of people.

The first stage of Jesus' ministry was reaching out to the nation of
Israel as the Savior, the Messiah. In Matthew 15:24, Jesus said, "I was
sent only to the lost sheep of the house of Israel." However, in today's
Bible reading Jesus told the Syrophoenician woman that the children
(Israel) deserve the bread (healing and ministry), but he responded
to her pleading. She begged Jesus by saying that even the dogs
(which represent the Gentiles in this case) get to eat crumbs that fall
from the table. Jesus responded by setting her daughter free from an
unclean spirit.

The story of the Syrophoenician woman is a foretaste of the second stage of ministry to the Gentiles. According to Mary Ann Tolbert
(*Sowing the Seed of the Gospel*), chapters 11-16 of Mark are based
around the parable of the vineyard (12:1-12). In this parable, God

plants a vineyard, leases it to tenants (Israel), and sends servants (the prophets) to collect from the tenants. The tenants mistreat every servant. Finally, we read what happens when God sends his beloved son to them: "But those tenants said to one another, 'This is the heir, come, let us kill him, and inheritance will be ours.' So they seized him, killed him, and threw him out of the vineyard. What then will the owner of vineyard do? He will come and destroy the tenants and give the vineyard to others" (Mark 12:7-9).

Those who are outsiders to your ministry as a congregation are important to God. When Jesus entered the temple on Palm Sunday, he said, "Is it not written, my house shall be a house of prayer for all the nations?" (Mark 11:17). The Great Commission charges the church to "Go therefore and make disciples of all nations" (Matthew 28:19). As you pray for others, you can begin to make this vision a reality within your congregation by listening to the Holy Spirit to learn who the "outsiders" may be in your setting. For some congregations, this may mean a prison or jail ministry. For others, this may mean a Twelve Step ministry. For still others, it may mean outreach to people of other ethnic groups. Wait on God, listen to the Holy Spirit, and pray for open hearts in the outsiders to whom you are called to minister.

REFLECT

An excellent study can be done on outsiders by looking at the Bible texts that focus on "all nations." This evangelical theme is evident in both the Old and New Testaments.

1. Read Matthew 28:18-20; Mark 16:19-20; Luke 24:44-49; and Acts 1:1-8. To whom are we sent to bear witness to the gospel? What plan may God be showing you to carry out this mission?

2. Isaiah 66:18-23 states that God will "gather all nations and tongues." How can God carry out this vision in your congregation? In your community, who has your congregation overlooked? Create a list of people. What needs to happen to enable your congregation to be intentional in its outreach to these outsiders? How could they be transplanted into the life of your congregation?

RESPOND

The Syrophoenician woman was passionate for the deliverance of her daughter. For whom are you passionate? How may God be calling you to respond?

Mark 7:31-37

Those Who Seek Healing

READ

The more a gardener considers a plant's needs for growth, the more productive the plant will be. A good gardener plans ahead to meet the spacing needs of full-grown plants. Some plants that appear small when started indoors, such as cucumbers, will need much more room when they spread out later. Gardeners must also consider the amount of space needed for what cannot be seen— the growth of roots.

Mary* had spinal damage since birth. She had worn a back brace her whole life, but now as she was nearing 30, increasing pain and other physical problems meant that she would soon face a high-risk surgery or be confined to bed. On many occasions, Mary's congregation prayed for her and this gave her strength. She felt loved and cared for by the congregation.

Surgery was the option Mary chose. As she waited for the scheduled date, a congregation of another denomination offered a healing service to the community. Out of desperation, Mary went to this healing service. She was instantly healed that night and no longer needed her brace or the surgery! Mary was so excited and filled with the love of God that she overflowed in enthusiasm. She spoke words of praise and wonder to God in her congregation the next Sunday. After 30 years of wearing a brace and dealing with restrictions in her life, she could not stop praising and talking about this miracle of God. By the month's end, the congregation council held a discussion and voted to remove Mary from membership because she was a "troublemaker" and had caused many members to be uncomfortable.

---

* Although the name has been changed, this story is based on actual events.

A healing ministry has always been a part of the church. First, Jesus ministered to the needs of many who were very ill or facing disabilities, such as the man who was deaf and had difficulty speaking (Mark 7:31-37). The disciples also were instructed, empowered, and sent to proclaim the kingdom of God and to heal (Mark 6:6-13). Today, many congregations offer occasional services of healing.

The Bible says that we are to pray for those in need. It is God who heals and we simply entrust each person into God's hands. We must admit that we do not understand why some are completely healed, many experience some improvement in health, and many others experience the gift of being prayed for but do not receive improved health.

How does your congregation welcome and reach out to people who have disabilities? In the 2000 U.S. census, people with disabilities numbered approximately 45 million, approximately 20 percent of the U.S. population. This includes people with physical disabilities, developmental disabilities, and mentally illnesses. There may be much good soil here, but it often gets overlooked or ignored by congregations.

REFLECT

A number of the daily exercises have focused on the healing stories of Jesus. Hearing these stories can be painful to those facing the challenges of disabilities. They may fear that they will not know how to deal with it if they receive prayers for healing and nothing seems to happen. It must be stated up front that it is God who heals or chooses not to heal at this time.

1. Christian Healing Ministries, led by Francis and Judith MacNutt, encourages the practice of "soaking prayer." Just as dry ground benefits from a lengthy soaking rain, one who is sick can be showered in continual soaking prayer by those who are interceding for that person. Who might you want to soak in prayer? As often as these people come to your mind each day, soak them in prayer, asking God to heal and bless them.

2. Jesus accepted people as they were and continued to lead them to deeper lives in God's presence. How does your congregation model acceptance of all people where they are? Do you have designated parking, an accessible worship space and rest rooms, and so on for those who are in wheelchairs? Are there accommodations for the hearing impaired or visually impaired? Do you involve people in praying for others who have physical disabilities? How could your congregation respond?

RESPOND

Does your congregation offer periodic services of healing? If so, are these healing services advertised to the community? If you do not currently offer healing services, could this be something that God is leading you to consider?

Mark 10:46-52

Bold Bartimaeus

READ

Certain plants benefit from special attention. With A-frame trellises, poles, and chicken-wire fences to climb and support them, plants such as pole beans, tomatoes, and cucumbers produce better.

The more that congregations demonstrate openness to the movement and direction of the Holy Spirit, as well as sensitivity to the needs of all people and compassion to those who are hurting, the more they will reflect the spirit of Christ.

Have you ever walked by someone begging and pretended not to notice? As Jesus passed through Jericho en route to Jerusalem, Bartimaeus was both bold and persistent in shouting out to him. Bartimaeus was not going to be "shushed" by anyone. In this beggar, Jesus encountered good and receptive soil.

Note that when Bartimaeus came to Jesus, the Lord asked him, "What do you want me to do for you?" Bartimaeus said, "My teacher, let me see again" (Mark 10:51). Jesus' question addresses two important points regarding prayer. The first is the value of being clear about what it is we are seeking in our prayers. The second point is that Jesus did not assume to know what Bartimaeus wanted. He asked a question instead. We too need to ask other people how we can pray for them as intercessors. Even if the type of prayers needed seem obvious to you, ask the person for his or her prayer requests. You might be surprised by the answer.

Bartimaeus is the final example of good soil in Mark's Gospel. Once left out on the edge of the community, Bartimaeus is healed and allowed to join Jesus on the way to Jerusalem.

REFLECT

The healing of the blind man named Bartimaeus encourages us to be bolder in our requests to God. There may be some around us who attempt to shush us too. Remember that Bartimaeus then "cried out even more loudly" (10:48).

1. Pray the story of Bartimaeus: Read the story several times and then pray the story from the perspective of Bartimaeus, the crowd, and Jesus. What comes to your mind as you pray?

2. Who is the Bartimaeus in your community—a person you may have ignored because you were too busy walking with Jesus, just like the crowd? Who has your congregation failed to notice as good soil—someone simply needing the invitation to come and worship Jesus? What about those who were once faithful worshipers and workers in the ministry of the congregation but no longer attend, perhaps because of some type of hurt in the past? How can you best pray for these people?

RESPOND

What kind of soil is in your heart? How is God calling you to pray for this soil?

Pray the prayer in Ephesians 1:17-19 several times. What is God showing you about yourself, about your congregation, and about the needs of people in your community? What will you do in response to these discoveries?

Prayer Covenant

In response to the call of Jesus to pray, I commit myself to a minimum of 15 minutes of prayer each day. I commit to participating in each of the small group sessions, following a daily discipline of prayer and study based on *Grounded in Prayer*, and praying for each person in my small group each day. I am making this covenant with God and my prayer group.

Signed: _____

Date: _____

Small Group Members and Information

Name	Phone Number	E-mail Address